WORDS

Integrated Decoding and Spelling Instruction Based on Word Origin and Word Structure

Second Edition

Marcia K. Henry

PRO-ED, Inc.
An International Publisher
8700 Shoal Creek Boulevard
Austin, Texas 78757-6897
800/897-3202 Fax 800/397-7633
www.proedinc.com

© 1990, 2010 by PRO-ED, Inc.
8700 Shoal Creek Boulevard
Austin, Texas 78757-6897
800/897-3202 Fax 800/397-7633
www.proedinc.com

ISBN: 978-1-4164-0441-5

Art Director: Jason Crosier
Designer: Vicki DePountis
This book is designed in Avant Garde, Minion Pro, and Chalkboard.

Printed in the United States of America

6 7 8 9 10 19 18 17

Contents

Overview v

Pretest 1

Unit 1 Lessons
Organizing Letter-Sound Correspondences **7**

Unit 2 Lessons
Syllable Patterns **57**

Unit 3 Lessons
Layers of Language: Anglo-Saxon, Latin, Greek **89**

Unit 4 Lessons
Morpheme Patterns **131**

Unit 5 Lessons
Strategies for Decoding and Spelling Long, Unfamiliar Words **181**

Unit Quizzes 221

Posttest 227

Non-Phonetic Words 233
- List 1
- List 2

Assorted Word Lists 235
- Words of Latin Origin
- Words of Greek Origin
- Words for Lesson 5.1
- Science and Social Studies Words for Lesson 5.2

Content Area Words for Lesson 5.3
Prefixes Expressing Number

Spelling Rules 239
Silent *e*
ff, ll, ss, zz
Soft *c* and *g*
ck, tch, dge
Adding Suffixes
Syllable Division
Plurals

Resources 243

References 245

Overview

Research Base

In the past 20 years, since the first publication of *Words*, new research has converged on the importance of explicit, systematic instruction in reading. The National Reading Panel (2000), which was formed to summarize research and implications for effective instruction, recommended five areas of instruction:

- Phonological awareness
- Phonics
- Fluency
- Vocabulary
- Comprehension

McCardle and Chhabra (2004) summarized a great deal of the reading research supported by the National Institute of Child Health and Human Development (NICHD). Research shows that students who are poor readers in first grade are generally poor readers in upper elementary school (Mathes et al., 2005; Shaywitz, 2003). The need for a program such as *Words*—which emphasizes decoding and its counterpoint, spelling, beyond the primary grades—provides opportunities for struggling readers to gain the literacy skills needed for success in school and in the community. Both accurate reading and accurate spelling require knowledge of several components of language, including phonology (the sound system), orthography (the spelling system), morphology (the structure of forms of words), and etymology (the history and origin of words; Henry, 2003; Silliman, Bahr, & Peters, 2006).

Knowing the common patterns contained in single and multisyllabic words enhances not only decoding and spelling, but also fluency, vocabulary, and comprehension. Ehri (2004) reported that systematic and explicit instruction in phonics is the most effective way to ensure appropriate reading growth in students. Learning phonics for single syllables, along with learning syllable division and morpheme patterns (the meaning units, such as compound words, prefixes, suffixes, Latin roots, and Greek combining forms), provides strategies for decoding and spelling unfamiliar words (Henry, 2003). In addition, learning the common morphemes enhances vocabulary and comprehension.

New forms of service delivery have also been introduced since the original version of *Words*. Response to Intervention (RTI) and differentiated instruction seek to identify struggling readers early and provide appropriate intervention as soon as possible (Berninger & Wolf, 2009). *Words* can be used as both Tier 1 and Tier 2 interventions or in Tier 3 or special education settings.

The *WORDS* Program

Words is designed for teachers of children and adults with reading-spelling skills of approximately third-grade level and above. Children in either general education or learning disability classrooms will benefit from this material meant to supplement traditional classroom reading instruction. Lessons are planned for classroom or small-group instruction, but they can also be used with individual students. Torgesen (2004) and Vaughn and Linan-Thompson (2003) found that struggling readers are served as well in small groups of three to four students as they are individually.

The instructional approach found in these materials emphasizes decoding and spelling instruction based on word origin and word structure. Earlier research using this approach showed that understanding word structure enhances word structure knowledge as well as decoding and spelling ability (Henry, 1988). The instructional process follows procedures used in Orton-Gillingham (Gillingham & Stillman, 1956) and Project READ (Calfee & Henry, 1986) programs.

Students and teachers focus on the content, structure, and process of the lesson in well-defined openings, objectives, procedures found in middle activities, and closings. Lessons center on specific spelling patterns and rules (content), pattern placement and word features (structure), and reading and spelling of numerous words fitting the target pattern (process). Thus, students may be learning about (a) the Latin root words *tract, spect,* and *dict* (content) and (b) their orthographic features and location in words (structure) as they (c) generate additional words, read word lists with numerous examples, and spell words from dictation (process). Follow-up activities enable reinforcement of the patterns or concepts.

Words provides teachers with "scripts" for developing generic openings, procedures, and closings for integrated decoding and spelling instruction. These scripts are only guidelines for what is being taught. Teachers should use the terminology with which they are familiar.

Table O.1

Word Origin by Word Structure Matrix

WORD ORIGIN	LETTER-SOUND CORRESPONDENCES	SYLLABLE PATTERNS	MORPHEME PATTERNS
ANGLO-SAXON	**Consonants** *sad* *stand* *thin* **Vowels** *cap/cape* *card* *boil* *pin/pine* *tall* *foul*	**Closed:** *mad* **Open:** *hobo* **VC*e*:** *kite* **Vowel digraph** or **vowel team:** *bead* **C–*le*:** ramble ***R*-controlled:** *barn, bird*	**Compound** *cowboy* *software* **Affix** *like* *get* *unlike* *forget* *unlikely* *forgetting*
ROMANCE based on LATIN	**Schwa (ə) prevalent** *direction* *spatial* *excellent*	**Closed:** *struct, flect, rupt* **VC*e*:** *scribe, vene* ***R*-controlled:** *port, form*	**Affix** *construction* *erupting* *conductor*
GREEK	*ch* for /k/ – *chorus, scholar* *ph* for /f/ – *phonograph* *y* as /i/ – *symphony* Also – *pn, ps, pt, mn, rh*	**Closed:** *graph, gram* **Open:** *photo, micro* **Unstable digraph:** *create*	**Compound** *microscope* *hemisphere* *metropolis*

Note. V = vowel; C = consonant. From *Understanding English Orthography: Assessment and Instruction for Decoding and Spelling* (Doctoral dissertation, Stanford University), by M. K. Henry, 1988, Dissertation Abstracts International, 48,11, p. 35. Copyright 1987 by Marcia K. Henry.

The model supporting the instruction is presented as a word origin by word structure matrix (see Table O.1). The matrix represents the categories of word structure (letter-sound correspondence, syllable, and morpheme) and of word origin (Anglo-Saxon, Latin, and Greek). The goal is to make students keenly aware that words of different origins may have different patterns. For example, words of Greek origin add new letter-sound correspondences, such as *ch* as in *chorus*, *ph* as in *phonograph*, and *y* as in *symphony*. The patterns (letter-sound correspondences, syllables, and morphemes) become the strategies available to decode unfamiliar words. Good readers first look for familiar morphemes in unknown words, and then they make decisions based on syllable division. Only when these two strategies have been applied do they rely on letter-sound associations. Beginning or poor readers, on the other hand, appear to use only one strategy: They "sound out" the word letter by letter-sound. While this approach may work for short, regular, one-syllable words, it furnishes little help for reading longer words.

Understanding how these patterns are influenced by word origin (words of Anglo-Saxon, Latin, and Greek origin make up the majority of English words) adds yet another useful dimension for reading and spelling unknown words. For example, when attempting the unknown word *interruption*, the reader will be able to recognize the Latin prefix, root, and suffix. As *-tion* has a unique pronunciation, knowing this suffix makes decoding thousands of words possible. Understanding these forms is equally beneficial for spelling. The speller may be tempted to write "interupshun," but knowing that the prefix *inter-* ends with an *r* and that the root *rupt* begins with an *r*, he or she is less likely to omit an *r*. Additionally, knowing that the suffix /shən/ is usually spelled *-tion*, the student is able to write the word correctly.

The Units

Before beginning the units, the *Words* Pretest may be given to assess students' knowledge of the terminology and concepts to be taught. Following each unit, the corresponding quiz may be administered to assess students' learning. After completing all five *Words* units, the Posttest may be given.

In each of the scripted lessons, teachers open by describing the purpose and objectives of the lesson and by presenting the new content, generally one or more patterns within a structural category. For example, in order to familiarize students with consonant digraphs, teachers may (a) focus on the similarities and differences of words containing four digraphs, (b) have students read a list of words with consonant digraphs on the board arranged in four separate columns, (c) ask students to generate new words for the four columns, (d) dictate words for spelling, and (e) assign children to look for words containing consonant digraphs in their reading books.

Students have many opportunities to use each new concept for both reading and spelling. The lessons allow the students to think of each concept and strategy as a problem-solving activity. For example, students might be asked to make decisions about whether or not final consonants in a number of words are doubled when adding various suffixes.

Lessons end with a review of the content, structures, and process just covered. Teachers encourage students to reflect upon what they have learned and to review the key ideas. Follow-up assignments may suggest that students identify and use target patterns found in newspapers, literature, or content area textbooks. Follow-up assignments also include a student handout for each lesson. Unit quizzes assess what has been learned and what needs to be reviewed.

One goal of this instruction is to allow students to transfer their new knowledge when decoding and spelling unfamiliar words. The lessons also provide students with a way to talk about decoding and to monitor their performance.

The materials are organized into five units related to the word origin/word structure matrix. The notion of word origin from a historical perspective flows through each unit. The design and sequence of the instructional units remain the same for all students, although patterns and words selected for practice may differ with grade level. The lessons are not meant to be comprehensive for each category, but are meant to organize prior information and present new material in a coherent way.

The five units of instruction focus on the following:

Unit 1: Organizing Letter-Sound Correspondences

Unit 2: Syllable Patterns

Unit 3: Layers of Language: Anglo-Saxon, Latin, Greek

Unit 4: Morpheme Patterns

Unit 5: Strategies for Decoding and Spelling Long, Unfamiliar Words

Units contain 10 to 14 lessons. The first lesson provides an introduction, and the last contains a review. Teachers may want to subdivide some lessons, depending on students' needs and on time availability.

In Unit 1, students organize the letter-sound correspondences they may have studied in the primary grades. In Unit 2, students consider syllable patterns. Unit 3 introduces students to the layers of language (Anglo-Saxon, Latin, and Greek) influencing English. Unit 4 provides numerous opportunities to read and spell words with Latin- and Greek-based morphemes. In Unit 5, students practice using alternative strategies for decoding and spelling long, unknown words, many of which can be found in their content area textbooks.

Table 0.2
Basic Anglo-Saxon Letter-Sound Correspondences

CONSONANTS		
Single Letters	Blends	Digraphs
b, c, d, f, g, h, j, k, l, m, n, p, q, r, s, t, v, w, x, y, z	**Initial:** *bl, cl, fl, gl, pl, sl* *br, cr, dr, fr, gr, pr, tr* *sc, sl, sm, sn, sp, st, tw* *scr, str, spl, spr . . .* **Final:** *ct, ft, lf, lk, lp, mp,* *nd, nt, sk, st, xt . . .*	**ch:** *chip, peach, church* **sh:** *shame, crash* **th:** *this, thick, that* **th:** *thin, thick* **wh:** *which, whale* **Also:** *wr, kn, gn, ck, tch, dge, ng . . .*
VOWELS		
Single Letters (Short/Long)	*R-* & *L-*Controlled	Digraphs
a – cap/cape *e – pet/Pete* *i – pin/pine* *o – rot/rote* *u – cut/cute* *w – cow/few* *y – gym/my, baby*	*ar – barn, parish* *arr – marry* *or – for, corn* *er, ir, ur – her, perish, bird, hurt* *err – berry* *ear – bear, fear, learn* ***l*-controlled** – *wall, halter, full*	**1 sound:** *ai & ay – nail, play* *ee – feed* *oa – coat* *oy & oi – boy, foil* *aw & au – cause, draw . . .* **2 sounds:** *ea – bead, head* *ei – either, vein* *ie – tie, grief* *oo – room, book* *ou – loud, boulder* *ow – brown, blow . . .*

Note . . . = additional blends and digraphs not listed. From *The Book: Components of Reading Instruction* (Unpublished manuscript) (p. 25), by R. C. Calfee and Associates, 1981, CA: Stanford University. Copyright 1981 by R. C. Calfee and Associates. Adapted with permission.

Unit 1: Organizing Letter-Sound Correspondences

The first unit introduces students to the structures inherent in letter-sound correspondences. Students learn terminology and organize their prior decoding knowledge according to a 2 × 3 matrix focusing on consonant and vowel patterns (see Table O.2). This matrix represents the way letter-sound correspondences can be organized for instruction. Students learn that words have both consonants and vowels, the two major headings. Consonants are single letters, blends, or digraphs. Single-letter vowels can have either short or long sounds, often lose their traditional sound when followed by *r* or *l*, and are called *vowel digraphs* when combined with other vowels. Almost all graphemes (the letter patterns appearing in words) can be placed in one of these six cells. This makes it possible to organize within a coherent framework the almost 200 isolated patterns found frequently in words of one or more syllables (Calfee & Associates, 1981).

Since the material in the *Words* manual is written for older elementary children, this letter-sound-correspondences matrix is used to review and organize their prior phonics knowledge. However, if you are using the material with younger students (i.e., those in Grades 2 and 3), the matrix can be used to introduce and organize letter-sound correspondences. Make a blank six-cell matrix and add consonant and vowel patterns to the blank cells as they are introduced. In addition to learning the patterns in each category, students will explicitly learn the terminology specific to word features. (NOTE: If you use different terms to describe the same patterns, use those terms. For example, in some instructional materials, *consonant blends* are called *consonant clusters,* and *vowel digraphs* are called *vowel teams.)*

As children learn the various letters and letter combinations, both print and cursive writing instruction should be included. Careful monitoring of letter formation by the teacher is encouraged.

Unit 2: Syllable Patterns

Students begin by discussing the meaning of the term *syllable* and practice counting the number of syllables in words of two to five syllables. Students learn about the six common syllable types and learn about both simple and complex syllable-division patterns existing in most multisyllabic words. Students read long words and divide them into syllables. They also spell words, being sure to count the syllables before writing and to say each syllable as they write.

Unit 3: Layers of Language: Anglo-Saxon, Latin, Greek

Students study how different word origins influence word structure and therefore English orthography. Teachers discuss the growth of written language, tracing the link of picture drawing, pictographs, and ideograms to alphabetic writing. They then describe the events contributing to the formation of English.

Letter-sound correspondences, as well as syllable and morpheme patterns, are contrasted for each layer of language. Anglo-Saxon letter-sound correspondences, syllable patterns, and morpheme patterns that consist of compound words and affixes, as well as common but irregular words, are considered. Next, the schwa sound (prevalent in words of Latin origin) is introduced, followed by common prefixes, suffixes, and roots. Teachers also introduce their students to the patterns prevalent in Greek-based words.

Unit 4: Morpheme Patterns

Meaning-based morphemes make up thousands of English words. This unit focuses primarily on Latin-based prefixes, roots, and suffixes. Prefixes introduced include *re-, pre-, de-, pro-, mis-, trans-, ex-, uni-, inter-,* and *intro-*. Among the suffixes taught are *-ist, -ant, -ent, -ible, -or, -tion, -tious, -cial, -cian,* and *-sion.* Latin roots include *rupt, form, tract, script, spect, struct, dict, flect, fer,* and *mit/miss.* Students also focus on Greek combining forms (often called *roots)* such as *auto, phono, hydro, hyper, chron, micro, hemi, graph, meta,* and *sphere.* Students are given opportunities to read and spell numerous words and to generate new words fitting each category. Learning morphemes enhances not only decoding and spelling, but vocabulary development as well.

Unit 5: Strategies for Decoding and Spelling Long, Unfamiliar Words

In this unit, students synthesize the information from previous units. Students practice using their new skills as they analyze long, unfamiliar words. Students follow the sequence used by most fluent readers: They first check for affixation and roots (morphemes). Next, they divide words into syllables. Only if these two strategies fail do they use letter-sound correspondences. In spelling, they are taught to first repeat the word, listen for syllables, and try to identify common affixes and roots. Students are encouraged to use letter-sound correspondences only after they attempt the morpheme and syllable strategies. They review productive spelling rules (i.e., rules for adding suffixes) to assist in spelling words from dictation.

Lesson Procedures

A Pretest is included to check students' prior knowledge about the structure of the English language and their word recognition and spelling ability. Feel free to skip lessons in which students are already proficient.

Lessons within each unit focus on specific patterns within the historical and structural categories. Teachers first introduce students to the structural or conceptual focus of the unit. In the lessons that follow, students continue to learn and practice new concepts related to each pattern. The final lesson reviews and summarizes the unit.

The decoding lessons are designed to be presented in five units of 10 to 14 consecutive lessons, which take approximately 45 minutes each to complete. Some teachers teach the lessons on a daily basis for a 10-week period, while others teach the decoding lessons two to three times weekly for an entire semester. Still others expand each lesson and use the units throughout the school year.

Although teachers spend different amounts of time on the lessons, teachers should follow the lesson sequence and format as designed. Each lesson consists of the "opening," in which the teacher describes the purpose and content of the lesson and explains the lesson procedures. Teachers read the red text to students. Following the opening, the teacher provides one or more "middle activities." These activities are framed in a small-group discussion format; students have the opportunity to read, spell, and discuss the patterns and concepts presented. Middle activities provide numerous examples of words fitting each pattern or rule, although some teachers delete some of the words during instruction, depending on their students' reading levels. Lesson plans for several lessons suggest optional word lists and activities, and many teachers include these in the lessons. Students also have the opportunity to generate new words.

At the end of each lesson, teachers and students review and summarize the concepts and patterns learned each day. This "closing" is an important facet of any lesson. During the closing, students and teachers discuss the lesson in terms of its content, relationship to other patterns, key terminology, and applicability to their reading and spelling.

Follow-up activities are found in handouts associated with each lesson. Students may be assigned the handouts as independent work following a lesson, or the handouts may be completed later as homework. Student handouts are found on the accompanying CD and can be printed and photocopied for student use. Each handout provides reinforcement and practice for concepts in each lesson. Reduced-size answer keys can be found in this manual at the end of each lesson. Encourage students to answer the questions on the handouts and to review concepts when needed.

Additional follow-up activities are also suggested in many lessons. Students might be asked to underline words containing Latin word roots in a newspaper article or to find as many Greek words as possible in a chapter of their science textbook.

Administer the Unit Quizzes at the end of each unit. They can be found on the CD and may be printed and photocopied. Directions, along with the Word Recognition and Spelling Dictation sections, can be found at the end of this manual. Try not to use the dictation words in your instruction, if possible. Reduced-size answer keys are also at the end of the manual.

Use the Posttest (found after the Unit Quizzes) to evaluate students' achievement at the end of the *Words* program. Return to and review any concepts students have not learned.

Materials

This revised *Words* program includes a manual and a CD-ROM. The manual contains the teaching materials, and the CD-ROM stores the reproducible tests, quizzes, and student handouts, as well as supplemental word lists and an overview of common spelling rules.

At the end of each lesson in the manual, the corresponding handout for that lesson is shown in reduced size, complete with answers to the exercises. The Pretest, Posttest, and Unit Quizzes can be found in their own sections of the manual, along with reduced-size answer keys at the end of each. The remaining sections include Non-Phonetic Words, Assorted Word Lists, Spelling Rules, and Resources. The Non-Phonetic Words list contains those phonetically irregular words that must be memorized for both reading and spelling. The Assorted Word Lists contain subject matter terms and provide practice for longer words. Although the Spelling Rules are taught directly in various lessons, they are found summarized at the back of the manual. The Resources provide additional books and Web sites that may be helpful for your *Words* instruction.

The *Words* CD-ROM offers a convenient way to print blank handouts, tests, and quizzes for students. The word lists and spelling rules can also be printed from the CD-ROM. Open the Words.PDF file on the CD-ROM. This file opens in Adobe Acrobat Reader (if you do not have Adobe Acrobat Reader on your computer, you may download it free from www.Adobe.com). Use the table of contents to navigate to the pages or sections you wish to print. Choose *Print* from the PDF menu, type in the page range, and then choose *OK*.

Teachers may want to make or purchase drill cards with the common patterns that are introduced. Instead of writing words on the board, word lists can be written on flip charts or wall charts so they may be used more than once. Otherwise, a chalkboard, whiteboard, or overhead projector can be used to list words for discussion and reading.

Students use newspapers, content area textbooks, literature, the Internet, and other classroom materials for follow-up assignments. Each student needs a three-ring binder with lined paper to use for spelling dictation and writing assignments based on the *Words* patterns. They may also keep their handouts and word lists in their binder so they can refer to them if they need to.

Pretest

Directions for Teachers:

Ask students to fill in their first and last names, grade, and the date on the top of the Pretest.

Numbers 1–12: Word Structure

Tell students you will ask them to circle parts of the words listed in the first few sections of the test. Let them know that some words may not contain the target word part. (During the test, remind students not to circle the whole word, only the part requested.)

Have students find number 1 on the Pretest. Read aloud the first line following number 1 on the test as the students read along silently.

NOTE: Do not define the underlined words, although you may repeat the key phrase (e.g., the *consonants*). Also, do not read any of the words to the students. In many cases, they won't have to read the words to identify the word parts.

Give students 60–90 seconds to complete the section. Then point out number 2, read the directions, and give 60–90 seconds to complete number 2. Continue in this manner through number 12.

1. Circle the consonants in the following words:

bag	cup	tax	globe
summit	campus	yoga	Atlantic
inventor	sympathetic	examine	retrospective

2. Circle the vowels in the following words:

tap	vote	load	stack
pilot	hotel	grumpy	dislocate
conductor	evict	understandable	information

3. Circle any short vowels you find in the following words:

cup	note	crack	inch
jets	rumble	crisp	lobster
misspelled	dispute	submitted	sympathy

4. Circle any long vowels you find in the following words:

mice	rode	dine	dinner
predict	return	lilac	erupted
reproduce	promotion	tripod	hypodermic

5. Circle any blends you find in the following words:

spot	grade	frame	stove
snap	clash	planet	destructive
milk	strict	garnish	trident

6. Circle any consonant digraphs you find in the following words:

thick	crash	thin	church
whipped	smooth	silent	shift
whales	chirp	shortly	thermal

7. Circle any vowel digraphs you find in the following words:

coat	flew	cloud	draw
boil	deceive	author	steamy
soda	exclaim	sailboat	headache

8. Divide any compound words you find into two word parts:

airplane	cowboy	baseball	marble
flashlight	railroad	moonlight	touchdown
tugboat	household	firecrackers	pancake

9. Circle any prefixes you find in the following words:

inside	report	express	raccoon
subway	define	reminded	displayed
alone	untimely	forgotten	prediction

10. Circle the roots, or base words, in the following words:

asleep	belong	report	extracted
midnight	remove	performing	inspection
impulsive	dictation	conversion	evicted

11. Circle any suffixes you find in the following words:

older	mixing	gardener	milked
active	invention	joyous	slightly
musician	aloud	hopeful	collector

12. Draw a line between the syllables in these words:

mitten	gentle	tennis	omit
collect	coincidence	reminder	Atlantic
conversion	popcorn	vacation	interpret

Number 13: Word Recognition

Dictate the following words to be circled from among the four words next to each letter. Give 15–20 seconds per item. (Before *q*, notify students that the next four words are not real words; they are nonsense words.)

a. reality b. crushed c. expand
d. noisily e. beside f. gladly
g. friendly h. cultivate i. quiet
j. shady k. whistle l. through
m. return n. secretly o. favorable
p. speculative

Nonsense words:

q. brouch (/ou/ as in *out*) r. sprŏt (rhymes with *lot*) s. ŏstĭnlŏp
t. frŭnlăstĭc

Number 14: Spelling

Dictate the following words to be spelled by the students. Tell students you will read the word once, give it in a sentence, and say the single word again. Students should be reminded to look at you while you say the word. Give students 20–25 seconds to write each word on their Pretest next to the appropriate letter. (Before *n*, notify students that the next three words are not real words; they are nonsense words.)

a. crouch	Crouch under the table.	crouch
b. roast	We'll roast the turkey.	roast
c. retire	He will retire soon.	retire
d. untimely	She had an untimely accident.	untimely
e. dislike	I really dislike this book.	dislike
f. mistake	She made a big mistake.	mistake
g. underlined	Lexe underlined all the words.	underlined
h. supervise	The teacher can't supervise her students.	supervise
i. collector	Cole is a shell collector.	collector
j. photograph	Noah gave me the colored photograph.	photograph
k. often	Maeryn often watches TV.	often
l. rough	He drove on the rough road.	rough
m. doubtful	The outcome was doubtful.	doubtful

Nonsense words:

n. blīpe
o. ĕpwīt
p. năbkorsăn

Name: ______________________ Grade: _________ Teacher: __________________

1. Circle the consonants in the following words:

bag	cup	tax	globe
summit	campus	yoga	Atlantic
inventor	sympathetic	examine	retrospective

2. Circle the vowels in the following words:

tap	vote	load	stack
pilot	hotel	grumpy	dislocate
conductor	evict	understandable	information

3. Circle any short vowels you find in the following words:

cup	note	crack	inch
jets	rumble	crisp	lobster
misspelled	dispute	submitted	sympathy

4. Circle any long vowels you find in the following words:

mice	rode	dine	dinner
predict	return	lilac	erupted
reproduce	promotion	tripod	hypodermic

5. Circle any blends you find in the following words:

spot	grade	frame	stove
snap	clash	planet	destructive
milk	strict	garnish	trident

6. Circle any consonant digraphs you find in the following words:

thick	crash	thin	church
whipped	smooth	silent	shift
whales	chirp	shortly	thermal

7. Circle any vowel digraphs you find in the following words:

coat	flew	cloud	draw
boil	deceive	author	steamy
soda	exclaim	sailboat	headache

8. Divide any compound words you find into two word parts:

airplane cowboy baseball marble
flashlight railroad moonlight touchdown
tugboat household firecrackers pancake

9. Circle any prefixes you find in the following words:

inside report express raccoon
subway define reminded displayed
alone untimely forgotten prediction

10. Circle the roots, or base words, in the following words:

asleep belong report extracted
midnight remove performing inspection
impulsive dictation conversion evicted

11. Circle any suffixes you find in the following words:

older mixing gardener milked
active invention *or tion* joyous slightly
musician *or cian* aloud hopeful collector

12. Draw a line between the syllables in these words:

mitten gentle tennis omit
collect coincidence reminder Atlantic
conversion popcorn vacation interpret

13. For each group of four words, circle the word dictated by your teacher:

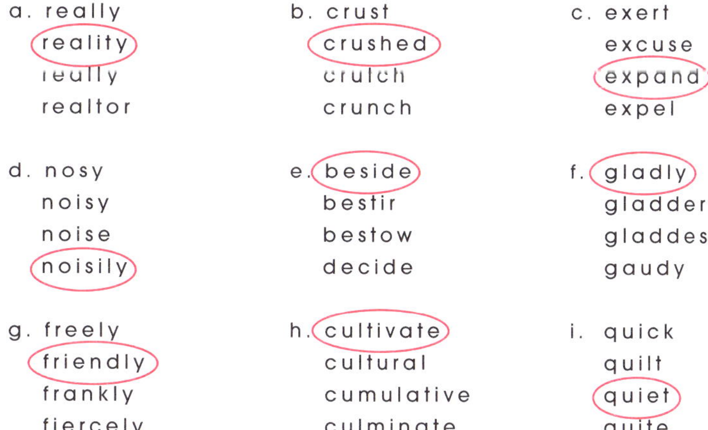

a. really reality really realtor
b. crust crushed crutch crunch
c. exert excuse expand expel
d. nosy noisy noise noisily
e. beside bestir bestow decide
f. gladly gladder gladdest gaudy
g. freely friendly frankly fiercely
h. cultivate cultural cumulative culminate
i. quick quilt quiet quite

Student Handout Answers

j. shabby
shady
shaggy
shade

k. weasel
thistle
frizzle
whistle

l. thorough
though
through
trough

m. retry
retreat
retire
return

n. security
secrecy
secretly
secretary

o. fashionable
favorable
favorite
favorably

p. spectacle
speculative
spectacular
speculate

q. brauch
brouch
broach
broich

r. sprit
spret
sprot
sprut

s. austinlup
ostinlop
awstinlip
ostinlap

t. funlastik
frunlastic
thunlastic
vunlastic

14. Spell the words as your teacher dictates them to you:

a. crouch
b. roast
c. retire
d. untimely
e. dislike
f. mistake
g. underlined
h. supervise
i. collector
j. photograph
k. often
l. rough
m. doubtful
n. blipe
o. epwit
p. nabkorsan *or* nabcorsan

Unit

1 Organizing Letter-Sound Correspondences

Lessons

1.1 Introduction to Organizing Letter-Sound Correspondences

1.2 Consonant Blends

1.3 Consonant Digraphs (*ch, th, sh, wh, ck* and Trigraphs *tch, dge*)

1.4 Consonant Digraphs (*wr, kn, gn, nk, ng*)

1.5 Comparing Consonant Blends and Consonant Digraphs

1.6 Two Additional Rules for Consonants

1.7 Short and Long Vowels and Vowel Markers

1.8 *R*-Controlled Vowels (*ar, or*)

1.9 More *R*–Controlled Vowels (*er, ir, ur*), Less Common *R*-Controlled Vowels, and *L*-Controlled Vowels

1.10 Vowel Digraphs (*ai, ay, ee, oa*)

1.11 Vowel Digraphs (*oi, oy, au, aw, ew, ue*)

1.12 Vowel Digraphs With Two Possible Sounds (*oo, ou, ow*)

1.13 Vowel Digraphs With Two Possible Sounds (*ea, ie, ei*)

1.14 Review of Letter-Sound Correspondences

Introduction to Organizing Letter-Sound Correspondences

In the next few weeks, we will be focusing on ways to help you read long and unfamiliar words. Five units will emphasize (1) common letter-sound correspondences, (2) syllable patterns, (3) how different languages influenced the English language, (4) morpheme patterns (those are things like prefixes, roots, suffixes, and compound words), and (5) strategies for reading and spelling long words. Many of the terms I just used are now unfamiliar to you. You will learn the meanings of all these terms and be able to understand the concepts they represent. In addition, you will have the chance to read and spell many new words.

NOTE: A small percentage of English words, most coming from the Old English period, are irregular (often called *non-phonetic words*), primarily in the vowel sounds. These are covered in Unit 3, Lesson 6. Common irregular words can be found in the Non-Phonetic Words lists of this manual, which can also be printed from the CD-ROM.

Opening

Our first task is to organize much of the information you already know. Over the past several years, you have learned many letters and their related sounds. That association of letters and sounds is often called *phonics.* Knowing about phonics is helpful for reading and spelling new words.

Objective

Students will organize this information and make a chart on the board.

NOTE: Although the order of examples may differ, the final chart will look something like the 2 x 3 matrix (Table O.2) in the Overview.

Procedure

Build the chart as you discuss the following:

Tell me the two kinds of letters that make up the alphabet. (*consonants and vowels*)

(If the response is "capital and lowercase," affirm, but tell students that both capital and lowercase letters can be broken down into consonants and vowels.)

We can divide consonants and vowels into three categories each. (Write categories on board as follows:

Table 1.1 Basic Anglo-Saxon Letter-Sound Correspondences

CONSONANTS		
Single Letter	Blends	Digraphs
VOWELS		
Single Letter Short/Long	*r*- & *l*-Controlled	Digraphs

Note. From *The Book: Components of Reading Instruction* (Unpublished manuscript), by R. C. Calfee and Associates, CA: Stanford University. Copyright 1981 by R. C. Calfee and Associates Adapted with permission.

Define the terms as you write in the labels. Write in one or two examples for each category.

Terms may differ slightly among reading programs. For example, some series call consonant blends *consonant clusters*. Others call vowel digraphs *vowel teams*. Use the terms with which you and the students are familiar.

NOTE: Some vowel digraphs are considered ***diphthongs*** (e.g., ***au, aw, oi, oy, ou, ow***) in other texts. Only the term ***vowel digraph*** will be used in this manual.

Terms

Consonants: All letters of the alphabet except *a, e, i, o,* and *u,* which are the vowels. (Point out that *y* and *w* are sometimes vowels (i.e., semivowels) when they appear in combination with another vowel (such as *ay* and *ow*).)

Single consonant: One consonant letter. (Most consonants have only one sound, though *c* and *g* each have a "hard" and a "soft" sound; *s* says both /s/ and /z/; and *x* has the /z/ sound in words of Greek origin.)

Blends: Two or three adjacent consonants in the same syllable that retain their individual sounds (e.g., *bl, dr, st, tw, mp, spr*). Blends may come at the beginning or end of a syllable.

Consonant digraph: Two adjacent consonants in the same syllable that have just one sound, often different from the sound of either letter (e.g., *ch, sh, th, wh, gn, ck* and trigraphs *tch* and *dge,* as well as *ng, wr,* and *kn*).

Vowel: The letters *a, e, i, o,* and *u. W* and *y* are sometimes found as semivowels in combination with another vowel, as in *aw, ew, ow, ay,* and *oy.* The letter *y* is a vowel at the end of words, as in *cry* and *baby.*

Short vowel sound: When vowels are in a *closed* position (i.e., followed by a consonant in a syllable), they have a *short* sound (e.g., *cat, fin, men, mop, hut*).

Long vowel sound: When vowels appear at the end of a syllable (as in *go, ho/bo, va/ca/tion*), or when they are *marked* with a vowel-consonant-*e* pattern (as in *make, Pete, time, coke, cute*), the vowels have a *long* sound, their own name.

***R-* and *l*-controlled vowel:** Vowels usually have neither a short nor a long sound when they are followed by *r* (e.g., *ar* in *park, chart; er* in *fern; ur* in *church*).

The letter *a*, when preceding *l*, has neither a short nor long sound (e.g., *all* in *tall; al* in *falter*).

Vowel digraph: Two adjacent vowels in the same syllable making one sound (e.g., *oa, ie, ai*).

NOTE: Some vowel digraphs are considered *diphthongs* (e.g., *au, aw, oi, oy, ou, ow*) in other texts. Only the term *vowel digraph* will be used in this manual.

Now, **write** a pattern on the board and see if students can identify the category. For example, if you write *ch*, students should identify that as a consonant digraph. If you write *oi*, students need to identify that as a vowel digraph.

Finally, ask children to name additional patterns for you to add to the blackboard chart. (If key patterns are missed, write them down and have students find the appropriate category.)

Closing

- What did we do today? *(Organized consonants and vowels into categories: Consonants (single, blend, digraph) and Vowels (short and long, r-and l-controlled, digraph); learned key terms; built a framework to organize phonics information and suggested words to fit each category)*

Review

- Read over the chart.
- Tell students that in the next decoding lesson they will work on consonant blends.

Follow-Up

- Provide a letter-sound correspondence chart in the room for reference.
- Have students complete the activities in Handout 1.1.

NOTE: Children with problems in auditory discrimination often have difficulty hearing the differences in certain pairs of consonants. These voiced and unvoiced consonants (often called *consonant pairs*) may be hard to differentiate for some students.

VOICED	UNVOICED
/b/ bat	/p/ pat
/d/ dug	/t/ tug
/g/ gut	/k/ cut
/j/ jug	/ch/ chug
/v/ vine	/f/ fine
/z/ zip	/s/ sip
/th/ that	/th/ thin
/w/ wail	/wh/ whale

Handout

1.1 Introduction to Organizing Letter-Sound Correspondences

Terms

Consonant: Any letter of the alphabet except *a, e, i, o,* and *u.*

Consonant blend: Two or three adjacent consonants in the same syllable that retain their individual sounds (e.g., *bl, dr, st, tw, mp, spr*). Blends may come at the beginning or end of a syllable.

Consonant digraph: Two adjacent consonants in the same syllable that have just one sound, often different from the sound of either letter (e.g., *ch, sh, th, wh, kn, gn, wr, nk, ng; tch* and *dge* are trigraphs).

Vowel: The letters *a, e, i, o,* and *u. Y* is sometimes a vowel, as is *w* in combination with another vowel (such as *aw* and *ow).*

Short vowel sound: Short vowels are found in *closed* syllables (i.e., followed by a consonant in a syllable). Examples include the vowels in *cat, fin, men, mop,* and *hut.*

Long vowel sound: Each long vowel has the sound of its own name. The vowel is long when it appears at the end of a syllable (as in *go, ho/bo, va/ca/tion*), or when it is marked with a vowel-consonant-*e* pattern (as in *make, Pete, time, coke, cute*).

***R-* and *l*-controlled vowels:** Vowels usually have neither a short nor a long sound when they are followed by *r* (e.g., *ar* in *park, chart; er* in *fern; ur* in *church*). The letter *a,* when preceding *l,* has neither a short nor a long sound (e.g., *all* in *fall; al* in *falter*).

Vowel digraph: Two adjacent vowels in the same syllable making one sound.

Activities

1. Circle the short vowels in the following words:

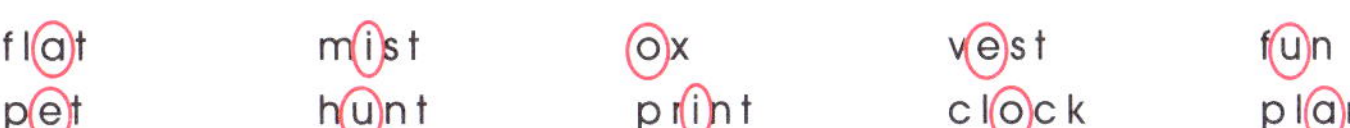

2. Circle the long vowels in the following words:

slope go drive grape cute
time crane flute so Pete

Student Handout Answers

3. Circle the consonant blends in the following words (some words may have more than one):

blast	milk	grime	blimp	flute
crab	stand	grove	blob	crust

4. Circle the consonant digraphs in the following words (some words may have more than one):

chip	whale	third	shake	knock
church	thin	shunt	when	wrist

5. Circle the vowel digraphs in the following words:

coin	flaunt	crow	bloom	south
plow	green	yeast	blew	glue

6. Circle the *r*-controlled vowels in the following words:

barn	fern	third	church	learn
chirp	chart	north	bear	girl

7. Read the following words:

fox	glad	pitch	spring	pond
drink	barn	skate	test	first

8. Use the words above to make complete sentences:

a. I'm ___glad___ the ___test___ is over.

b. ___Pitch___ the ball to the ___first___ baseman.

c. We ___skate___ on the frozen ___pond___ in winter.

d. ___Spring___ water is good to ___drink___.

Lesson 1.2 Consonant Blends

Opening

Today we will study consonant blends. You may remember that when two or three consonants are adjacent in the same syllable and retain their individual sounds, they are called consonant blends.

Objective

Students will read and spell numerous words containing consonant blends.

Procedure

Who can name some common blends? Write on the board. If students give a digraph, remind students of the definition, point out that each sound has to be heard and then blended together.

Write the following words on the board—keeping them in the columns shown—or write them in a flip chart (you may want to put all your word lists in flip charts so you can use them for review or use them year after year):

Ex: (sp)ot	Ex: le(ft)	Ex: (bl)a(st)
clap	silk	drift
blot	best	twist
flake	rust	blimp
slope	risk	swift
place	bend	spend
crib	melt	plump
dream	lump	stamp
stab	next	crust
sprain	hint	print
twin	sift	sprint
split	bulk	cramp
frill	help	brisk

Let's *read* the first column. Where are the blends? (*at the beginning of the words*) Circle the blends as students name them.

Let's *read* the second column. Where are the blends? (*at the end of the words*) Circle the blends as students name them.

Let's *read* the third column. Where are the blends? (*at the beginning and the end of the words*) Circle the blends as students name them.

Ask students to **spell** the following words containing blends. Dictate each word twice. Students should repeat the word, isolate the blend, then write the word while sounding it aloud. Be sure students check their spelling after writing each word.

jump	flask	milk	spent	film
stop	melt	spring	split	brisk

Dictate the following sentences for students to **spell:**

- Fred likes skim milk.
- Stan kept the sled near the ski jump.

Closing

- **What kind of patterns did we work on today?** (*consonant blends*)
- **Who can define a consonant blend?** (*two or three adjacent consonants in the same syllable that retain their individual sounds*)
- **Where do consonant blends come in words?** (*at the beginning, middle, or end*)
- **What did we do with consonant blends?** (*identified them; read and spelled words containing them*)

Follow-Up

- Have students look for consonant blends in their current basal story, literature book, or content area textbook.
- Ask students to complete Handout 1.2.

Handout

1.2 Consonant Blends

Reminders

Consonant blends are two or three consonants adjacent in the same syllable that retain their individual sounds. They can come at the beginning or end of syllables.

Common initial blends (those found at the beginning of syllables) include the following:

st, sm, sn, sl, sp, sc, sk, sw

bl, cl, fl, gl, pl

br, cr, dr, fr, gr, pr, tr, tw

spl, spr, scr, str

Common final blends (those found at the end of syllables) are as follows:

ft, ld, lk, lt, lp, mp, nd, nt, sk, sp, st

Activities

1. Circle the consonant blends in the following words. (Note that some words may not contain any consonant blends and some words may contain both initial and final blends.)

left	kite	lisp	swift	fit
hold	stump	crust	bath	flow
bulk	fast	chip	cramp	string

2. Use some words above to make complete sentences:

a. We ___held___ the ___kite___ by its long ___string___.

b. The ___fast___ runner had a ___cramp___ in his ___left___ leg.

Consonant Digraphs (*ch, th, sh, wh, ck* and Trigraphs *tch, dge*)

Opening

Today we will study consonant digraphs. You may remember that when two consonants are next to each other in the same syllable, and make a completely new sound, this combination is called a consonant digraph.

Objective

Students will read and spell numerous words containing consonant digraphs.

Procedure

What are some common consonant digraphs? Write responses on the board.

Write the following words on the board:

chop	hush	which
this*	bath	church
ship	hash	shush
white	with	
these	cash	
shake	wish	
thin	much	
chime	such	
whale	rich	

*The digraph *th* has two sounds: voiced, as in *this*, and voiceless, as in *thick*.

Have students **identify** placement of the digraphs: beginning, end, or both.

Ask students to **spell** several of the following words containing consonant digraphs. Dictate each word twice. Students should repeat the word, isolate the consonant digraph, then **write** the word while sounding it aloud. Be sure students check their spelling after writing each word.

when	chip	shop	while	white	bath
those	whale	church	chose	cash	shake

NOTE: The digraph *wh* is never used at the end of a word.

NOTE: Some reading materials and other texts call *ck, tch, dge, wr, kn, gn, nk,* and *ng* digraphs. We will consider *ck, tch,* and *dge* in this lesson and *wr, kn, gn, nk,* and *ng* in the following lesson.

Digraph *ck* and Trigraphs *tch* and *dge*

The digraph *ck* has the /k/ sound, *tch* has the /ch/ sound, and *dge* has the /j/ sound. Since *tch* and *dge* each have three letters, they are technically called *trigraphs.* All are used at the end of a one-syllable word directly following a short vowel. Have students **read** the words in each column. Ask them to look for the similarities in each column, such as ending in *ck* following a short vowel.

ck	***tch***	***dge***
back	fetch	ridge
sick	notch	grudge
clock	Dutch	bridge
truck	batch	dodge
fleck	stitch	badge
rock	stretch	dredge

Ask students to **spell** the following words from dictation:

brick	pitch	bridge	trudge
stack	flock	fetch	crutch

NOTE: The words *such, much, rich,* and *which* are common exceptions to the *tch* rule.

Ask students to **spell** the following sentences from dictation:

- The girl will pitch the ball under the ledge.
- Cross the bridge near the brick wall.

Closing

- **What pattern did we work on today?** (*consonant digraphs*)
- **Who can define a consonant digraph?** (*two adjacent consonants with a new sound*)
- **Where do they come in words?** (*beginning and/or end*)
- **What did we do with consonant digraphs?** (*identified them; read and spelled words containing them*)

Follow-Up

- Have students find consonant digraphs and trigraphs in their current reading books or in a content area textbook.
- Have students complete Handout 1.3.

Handout **1.3**

Consonant Digraphs (*ch, th, sh, wh, ck* and Trigraphs *tch, dge*)

Reminders

A consonant digraph is made of two adjacent consonants in the same syllable that make a completely new sound. Common consonant digraphs are *ch*, *sh*, *th*, and *wh*.

The two-letter combination *ck* is a digraph and the three-letter combinations *tch* and *dge* are trigraphs used at the end of a one-syllable word immediately after a short vowel. (*Such*, *much*, *rich*, and *which* are common exceptions.)

Activities

1. Circle any consonant digraphs or trigraphs you find in the following words:

cheer	whale	thirst	church	bath
grasp	chuck	this	whack	third
dodge	match	peach	chant	clip

2. Use some of the words above to make complete sentences:

a. The **whale** was bigger than the **bath** tub.

b. Give a **cheer** for the **third** baseman.

c. I like to play **dodge** ball at the **church** playground.

3. Read the following words:

peck	luck	stuck	flock	flick
milk	brick	beak	sulk	tack

a. Why don't *milk* and *sulk* require *ck?*

Both words have a consonant just before the final /k/ sound.

b. Why doesn't *beak* require *ck?*

Both words have two vowels just before the final /k/ sound.

4. Read the following words:

pitch	notch	lunch	ranch	match
pinch	batch	crutch	flinch	fetch
peach	patch	leech	pouch	crutch

a. Why don't *lunch, ranch, pinch,* and *flinch* require *tch*?

All five words have a consonant just before the final /ch/ sound.

b. Why don't *peach, leech,* and *pouch* require *tch*?

All three words have two vowels just before the final /ch/ sound.

5. Read the following words:

fudge	cage	bridge	strange	dodge
stage	fringe	ledge	pledge	grudge

a. Why don't *cage* and *stage* require *dge*?

Both words have a long vowel sound just before the final /j/ sound.

b. Why don't *strange* and *fringe* require *dge*?

Both words have a consonant just before the final /j/ sound.

Lesson 1.4 Consonant Digraphs (*wr, kn, gn, nk, ng*)

Opening

Today we will study other consonant digraph patterns. You may remember that when two consonants are next to each other in the same syllable, and make a completely new sound, this combination is called a consonant digraph.

Objective

Students will read and spell numerous words containing the consonant digraphs *wr, kn,* and *gn* (rare), as well as *nk* and *ng* words.

Procedure

What are some common consonant digraphs we studied earlier? Write on the board.

Today we will learn some new consonant digraphs.

Digraphs *wr, kn,* and *gn*

Write the following words on the board:

wrist	written	wrestle
wretch	wrote	write
wrap	wreck	wreath
wren	wriggle	wrench
wrecks	writhe	wrist
know	known	knack
knit	knife	knot
knave	knapsack	knee
knead	knew	knock
knits	gnash	gnat

NOTE: Both *wr* and *kn* come at the beginning of words; *gn* can come at the beginning or end of words.

Ask students to **spell** several of the following words containing *wr* and *kn*. Dictate each word twice. Students should repeat the word, isolate the consonant digraph, then **write** the word while sounding aloud. Be sure students check their spelling after writing each word.

write	knit	knot	wrote	knapsack	wrench
kneel	wreck	knife	wreath	wrath	know

Digraphs *nk* and *ng*

Unless vowels are placed in front of *nk* and *ng,* these letter combinations are difficult to pronounce. Teach the consonants with their preceding vowels (i.e., *ink, ank, onk, unk,* and *ing, ang, ong, ung,* and rarely *eng*).

Here are some words for you to read using *ink, ank, onk,* and *unk*:

ink	**ank**	**onk**	**unk**
sink	sank	honk	sunk
link	lank		hunk
wink	tank		chunk
stink	stank		stunk
drink	drank		drunk
think	thank		
brink			

Ask students to **spell** the following words from dictation:

crank	plank	think	drunk
honk	brink	thank	spank

Have students **spell** the following sentences from dictation:

- Thank your dad for the drink.
- Think about the pink tank top.

Here are some words to read using *ing, ang, ong, ung,* and *eng:*

ing	**ang**	**ong**	**ung**	**eng**
ring	rang	long	rung	length
sing	sang	song	sung	strength
sling	slang	strong	slung	
sting	gang	gong	stung	
string	clang	tongs	hung	
spring	sprang	wrong	sprung	
wring	bang		wrung	
thing			strung	

NOTE: The suffix *-ing* will be introduced in the morpheme section of the book (i.e., Lesson 3.5).

Ask students to **spell** the following words from dictation:

sting	song	stung	length
sprang	strong	sprung	string

Have students **spell** the following sentences from dictation:

- He sang the song about the bee sting.
- He strung the kite with long string.

Closing

- **What patterns did we work on today?** (wr, kn, gn, ink, ank, onk, unk, ing, ang, ong, *and* ung)
- **Who can define a consonant digraph?** (*two adjacent consonants with a new sound*)
- **Where do consonant digraphs come in words?** (*at the beginning and/or end*)
- **What did we do with consonant digraphs?** (*identified them; read and spelled words containing them*)

Follow-Up

- Have students complete Handout 1.4.

Handout 1.4

Consonant Digraphs (wr, kn, gn, nk, ng)

Reminders

Wr and *kn* are consonant digraphs found at the beginning of words (*gn* is rare, as in *gnat, gnash*, and *sign*). *Sh, th, wh, ch, ck, tch*, and *dge* were learned earlier.

Nk and *ng* follow consonants and are learned as separate patterns (e.g., *ink, ank, onk, unk; ing, ang, ong, ung*).

Activities

1. Read the words below and circle any consonant digraphs you find:

whish	knelt	thorn	quilt	shine
them	cheat	kneel	wrote	belt
knead	gnash	shift	cramp	church

2. Use some of the words above to make complete sentences:

a. Today I kneel down, yesterday I knelt.

b. He wrote the letter even with a thorn in his left hand.

3. Write at least 2 words in each column that contain the consonant digraphs shown:

ink	ank	onk (1 only)	unk
sink	bank	honk	hunk
think	sank		sunk
blink	thank		chunk

ing	ang	ong	ung
ring	sang	long	hung
thing	bang	song	clung
cling	clang	prong	sung

4. Read each word below. Change the *ink* to *ank, onk*, or *unk* to make a new word. Read the new word.

drink = drank or drunk
blink = blank
chink = chunk
clink = clank or clunk
sink = sank or sunk
stink = stunk

Student Handout Answers

5. Read each word below. Change the *ing* to *ang, ong,* or *ung* to make a new word. Read the new word.

sing = sang or sung
ring = rang or rung
sling = slang or slung
thing = thong
sting = stung
cling = clang or clung

Lesson

1.5 Comparing Consonant Blends and Consonant Digraphs

Opening

Today we will review the patterns known as *consonant blends* and *consonant digraphs*. We will compare and contrast the two patterns, and we will read and spell many words using blends and digraphs.

Objective

Students will compare and contrast consonant blends and consonant digraphs, and read and spell many words using the two patterns.

Procedure

Who can tell me the difference between a consonant blend and consonant digraph? Can you give me some examples? Probe and list on the board under category headings.

Can we have consonant blends and consonant digraphs in the same word? (*yes*)

Here are words containing both blends and digraphs. Let's read these words:

clinch	preach	splash
shift	thump	champ
chest	blush	flash

As students identify blends, circle the blend. As students identify digraphs, underline the digraph.

We can also have words in which digraphs are blended with consonants. Write the following words on the board.

Read the following words:

shrill	shrimp	thrash
thrush	thrift	shrub
bunch	thrush	lunch

Have students identify digraphs. Circle only the digraphs, not the consonant forming the blend (e.g., *shrill*).

NOTE: Older students should be aware that blends and digraphs can occur in the middle of longer words (e.g., *thrashing*—suffix added; *hundred; explosion,* etc.). However, the *mp* in *trumpet* and the *nd* in *candle* are not blends, and the *th* in *nuthouse* is not a digraph, as these consonants appear in different syllables.

For spelling practice, have students label two columns on their paper as follows:

Consonant Blends	**Consonant Digraphs**

Have students **write** words in the appropriate column as you dictate. Always have students repeat the word aloud after you say it. For example, words such as *blast, mist, clump,* and *flask* go in the Consonant Blends column and words like *that, chip, whale,* and *thatch* go in the Consonant Digraphs column.

Say (the spelling word). Students should repeat the spelling word.

Write it.

Check your own spelling.

Check it with mine. Write the word on the board.

Have students **spell** the following words as you dictate them:

Lower Grades	Upper Grades
gray	stripe
smile	twist
chop	thing
stripe	hundred
them	explode
whale	untwist
spend	whisper
twist	chilled
spoke	thirty
split	clasp
sprain	splendid
thing	thunder

Have students turn their paper over and **spell** the following words with both consonant blends and consonant digraphs:

Lower Grades	Upper Grades
thrust	thrust
trash	shiftless
thrill	shifty
blush	reproach
shift	shrimp
bunch	thrilling

Closing

- **What did we work on today?** (*the difference between consonant blends and consonant digraphs*)
- **Where are consonant blends and digraphs located in words?** (*at the beginning and/or end of one-syllable words, also the middle of longer words*)
- **What did we do during the lesson?** (*contrasted consonant blends and digraphs; read and spelled words containing blends and digraphs*)

Follow-Up

- Have students write complete sentences using words with consonant blends and consonant digraphs.
- Have students complete Handout 1.5.

Comparing Consonant Blends and Consonant Digraphs

Reminder

Many words contain both consonant blends and consonant digraphs.

Activities

1. Read the words below. Circle the consonant blends and underline the consonant digraphs.

French	clash	champ	brunch
twitch	whisk	splash	crunch
knelt	chest	splotch	thump

2. Insert one or two words from above to complete each sentence:

a. I had a twitch in my nose as I smelled the rose.

b. The boy knelt before the queen.

c. The boxing champ was hit in the chest.

d. I like French toast for brunch.

Lesson

1.6 Two Additional Rules for Consonants

Opening

You have already learned one rule for consonants: You know that we use *ck, tch,* and *dge* at the end of a one-syllable word immediately after a short vowel (e.g., *stick, match,* and *grudge*). There are two other important rules you need to know for consonants.

Objective

Students will learn that one-syllable words ending in *f, l, s,* and sometimes *z* usually double the final letter directly after a short vowel (e.g., *stuff, fill, grass, jazz*).

Students will learn that both *c* and *g* have two sounds. The "hard" sound of *c* is /k/, as in *cat, cot,* and *cut.* The "soft" sound of *c* is /s/, as in *city, ace,* and *cypress.* Note that *c* has the soft sound /s/ before *e, i,* and *y.* The hard sound of *g* is /g/, as in *gate, got,* and *gum.* The soft sound of *g* is /j/, as in *ginger, age,* and *gym.* Note that, like *c, g* has the soft sound (/j/) before *e, i,* and *y.*

Procedure

Ask students to **read** the following words and tell why the final letters are doubled:

grass	bless	dress	fill
still	tell	jazz	buzz
less	lass	hull	grill

NOTE: The phonogram *all*—as in the single word and in *tall, stall, mall,* etc.—also needs to be learned as a regular pattern.

Ask students to **read** the following words and decide if the *c* or *g* is hard or soft:

cell	call	got	gum
grim	clam	crib	cinch
cent	gem	glad	gent

NOTE: There are several common words that do not fit this rule. They include *girl, get, gift,* and *gill.*

Ask students to **spell** the following sentences from dictation:

- The boys got a cent for every glass they filled.
- Put the clams on the grill.

Closing

- **What new rules did we learn today?** (*double* f, l, s, *and* z; *soft and hard* c *and* g)
- **Who can give me the rule for using *ff, ll, ss,* and *zz*?** (*one-syllable words ending in* f, l, s, *and* z *after one short vowel will usually double the final consonant*)
- **Who can give me the rules for soft and hard *c* and *g*?** (c *and* g *have hard sounds before* a, o, *and* u *and all consonants and usually have soft sounds before* e, i, *and* y)

Follow-Up

- Have students complete Handout 1.6.

Handout

1.6 Two Additional Rules for Consonants

Reminders

One-syllable words ending in *l*, *f*, *s*, and sometimes *z* double the final *l*, *f*, *s*, and *z* directly after a short vowel.

The letter *c* usually has the /k/ sound but has the /s/ sound when it comes before *e*, *i*, and *y*.

The letter *g* usually has the /g/ sound but has the /j/ sound when it comes before *e*, *i*, and *y*.

Activities

1. Read the words below:

spice	city	catch	cult
place	voice	cell	cringe
count	center	clap	cent
clot	crust	clutch	cycle

2. Write the word in the first column if the *c* has the hard sound /k/; write the word in the second column if the *c* has the soft sound /s/.

c as /k/	*c* as /s/
catch	spice
cult	city
cringe	place
count	voice
clap	cell
clot	center
crust	cent
clutch	cycle

3. Read the words below:

gave	gym	ginger	gap
grasp	rage	guns	cringe
gem	gentle	glimpse	gypsy
glass	gust	germ	grange

4. Write the word in the first column if the *g* has a hard sound /g/; write the word in the second column if the *g* has the soft sound /j/.

g as /g/	*g* as /j/
gave	gym
gap	ginger
grasp	rage
guns	cringe
glimpse	gem
glass	gentle
gust	gypsy
gray	germ

Short and Long Vowels and Vowel Markers

Opening

Today we'll contrast long and short vowel sounds. We'll look for markers that give us information about whether the sound is short or long. We'll read and spell many words.

Objective

Students will identify short and long vowel markers and read and spell numerous words.

Procedure

Who remembers the five main vowels? (a, e, i, o, u)

Write the word *mad* on the board. Show the vowel-consonant (VC) pattern and remind students that when a vowel is followed by a consonant in the same syllable, the vowel is short. **Review** the short sounds of the five major vowels.

NOTE: The diacritical marking for the short vowel is the breve (˘). The diacritical marking for the long vowel is the macron (¯). Long vowels say their own names.

Write the following list of words on the board, and have students **read** the words:

List 1

mad
cap
mat
cut
Tim
hop
pan
hat
rat
hid
fat
tap
dim
fin
bit
rid

not
rod
win
tub
slim

Probe, **How are the words in this list alike?** (*VC pattern; short vowel; all one syllable*)

Next, rewrite the words in the first list, but add an e to each one (e.g., turn *mad* into *made*). The list should look as follows:

List 2

made
cape
mate
cute
time
hope
pane
hate
rate
hide
fate
tape
dime
fine
bite
ride
note
rode
wine
tube
slime

Have students **read** the words in List 2.

Probe, **How are the words in List 2 alike?** (*VCE pattern; long vowel; one syllable*)

How do the words in List 2 differ from the words in List 1? (*vowel sound*)

What is the marker for the long vowel sound? (*VCE, or final* e)

NOTE: You can point out that this marker works for longer words as well (e.g., *explode, vacate, populate, excite, include*).

Another marker is the doubled consonants that appear in many words.

Write the following words in a new list, and have students **read** the words:

List 1

pinning
batted
bitter
dinner
filling
holly
slopped
batting
latter
matting

Tell students that the doubled consonant cancels the long vowel signal that would otherwise be given by the *i* in *ing*, the *e* in *er* and *ed*, and the final *y*.

(A VCV pattern in the middle of two-syllable words usually gives us a long first vowel. This will be covered in Unit 2: Syllable Patterns.)

Write the following contrasting words in a second list, and have students **read** the words:

List 2

pining
bated
biter
diner
filing
holy
sloped
bating
later
mating

Ask students to contrast the two word lists. **Review** the role of the double consonant marker.

Now let's spell some words. Put words with short vowels in the first column on your paper and words with long vowels in the second column. Remember to use the markers we talked about as you spell the words. Listen for the vowel sounds. Be sure to repeat the word after I say it.

Have students **spell** the following words as you dictate them:

cut	dining	hop
time	dinner	hopping
cute	pinning	hoping
hope	grinned	vote
slope	thinner	inflate

Closing

- **What did we review today?** (*short and long vowels and vowel markers*)
- **What activities did we do?** (*read; spelled; contrasted short and long vowels*)

Follow-Up

- Ask students to look for vowel markers in their basal reader story, literature book, or a passage that you provide.
- Remind them of the markers as they write dictated sentences.
- Have students complete Handout 1.7.

Handout

1.7 Short and Long Vowels and Vowel Markers

Reminders

Vowels can be short or long. The diacritical marking for the short vowel is the breve (˘).

The diacritical marking for the long vowel is the macron (¯). Long vowels say their own names.

Vowel Markers for Short Vowels: Vowels are short when followed by one or more consonants at the end of a syllable (e.g., *mat, mist*). Vowels in words of more than one syllable will usually be short when two consonants divide the syllable (e.g., *thinner, gladness*).

Vowel Markers for Long Vowels: Vowels will be long with a final silent *e* at the end of a syllable (e.g., *slide, make*). Vowels in words of more than one syllable will usually be long when followed by a consonant and another vowel (e.g., *dining, final*).

Activities

1. Look at the list below. Mark short vowels with the breve (˘) and long vowels with the macron (¯).

flăt	chŭmp	vōte	fīve
cūbe	māde	slĭmmest	Frĕd
dīning	dĭnner	slŏp	slōpe

2. Cross out the word in each row below that does not belong:

slime	thine	slope	~~sled~~	crane
cutting	bigger	~~timing~~	sloppy	fitness
flat	~~slide~~	splat	crust	bench
cuter	~~fitting~~	dining	filing	making

R-Controlled Vowels (ar, or)

Opening

Today we'll discuss what happens to vowels when they are followed by the letter *r*. When vowels are followed by the letter *r*, the vowel rarely gets a short or a long sound. Instead, the vowel plus the letter *r* form a new sound.

NOTE: You may want to put most of the new or review patterns on 3 x 5-in. cards for rapid visual or auditory drills.

Objective

Students will read and spell numerous words with *ar* and *or* patterns.

Procedure

Have students **read** and **spell** words that fit each of the following patterns:

***ar* (as in *car*)**

car	tar	yarn	starlight	marching
bar	hard	starve	harness	harmless
jar	yard	partner	harvest	target
far	dark	mark	charming	carbon
star	barn	starch	bombard	garden
park	chart	larks	stardust	tarnish

***or* (as in *corn*)**

corn	pork	sport	forget	hornet
for	storm	stork	forgave	corner
fork	north	thorn	northwest	scorching
morn	porch	normal	orchard	morning
horse	morbid	forlorn	northern	fording

Have students **spell** the following sentences as you dictate them:

- We sat on the porch in the dark and watched the storm from the north.
- The large barn is next to the farmyard.

Closing

- **What new patterns did we learn today?** (ar *and* or)
- **What activities did we do?** (*read; spelled; contrasted* ar *and* or)

Follow-Up

- Have student look for *ar* and *or* words in literature books.
- Have students complete Handout 1.8.

Handout

1.8 R-Controlled Vowels (ar, or)

Reminders

Vowels followed by *r* in the same syllable do not have their standard short or long sound.

Ar has the sound found in words like *car*, *park*, and *star*.

Or has the sound found in words like *for*, *corn*, and *fork*.

Activities

1. Read the passage below and circle all the words containing *ar:*

   Carl parked the car next to the barn. The stars shone in the sky over the farm. It was hard to see the yard in the starlight with no moon. A lark sang in the dark.

2. Complete each sentence with a word from the word list below:

   harm scar shark sharp stars parked

   a. His ___scar___ was very sore.

   b. The ___shark___ will scare the swimmers.

   c. A bear with ___sharp___ claws will ___harm___ the hunters.

   d. The ___stars___ shine in the sky.

   e. He ___parked___ his Jeep near the house.

3. Read the passage below and circle all the words containing *or:*

   The short morning storm struck north of the border. Our horse barn and porch were hit by wind and hail.

4. Complete each sentence with a word from the word list below:

   corn short fort thorns order scorch

   a. Try not to ___scorch___ the ___corn___ as you cook it.

   b. The ___short___ dog ran around the old ___fort___.

   c. ___Order___ a new dress from the shop.

   d. Don't let the ___thorns___ stick you.

Lesson

1.9 R-Controlled Vowels (er, ir, ur), Less Common R-Controlled Vowels, and L-Controlled Vowels

Opening

In our last lesson, we discussed the *r*-controlled vowels *ar* and *or*. Today we'll discuss several other *r*-controlled vowels.

Objective

Students will learn *er, ir, ur* and several less common *r*-controlled vowels. They will also learn about *l*-controlled vowels.

Procedure

R-Controlled Vowels *er, ir, ur*

Tell students that *er, ir,* and *ur* all say the same /er/ sound, as in *her, bird,* and *fur.*

Have students **read** and **spell** words that fit each of the following patterns:

***er* (as in *fern*)**

fern	perch	jerk	stern	servant
her	berth	serf	tern	serge
term	verse	lantern	winter	merge

***ir* (as in *bird*)**

bird	birth	shirt	squirt	thirsty
girl	chirp	firm	squirrel	thirty
first	twirl	thirst	skirmish	confirm

***ur* (as in *nurse*)**

nurse	blur	turn	turtle	further
purse	sturdy	hurt	nursery	murder
church	curve	curl	purple	disturb
bust	urge	curly	hurling	churning

Less Common R-Controlled Vowels

Introduce the following less common *r*-controlled patterns. Have students **read** and **spell** these words:

ear /er/	***ear*** /air/	***er/err***	***ar/arr***
earn	bear	perish	parish
learn	wear	berry	garish
heard	pear	merry	barbarian
earth	tear		marry
rehearse			

L-Controlled Vowels

With the *l*-controlled vowel *a,* the letter a rarely gets a short sound before l. Write these words on the board and ask children to **read** them:

fall	call	halter
falter	tall	wall

Words containing the letter *u* followed by *ll* (e.g., *bull, pull,* and *full*) often must be memorized.

Closing

- **What are the major vowel *r* patterns?** (or, ar, er, ir, ur)
- **What are the common *l*-controlled vowels?** (al, all)

Follow-Up

- Have students look for *r*-controlled and/or *l*-controlled vowel patterns in their literature or textbooks.
- Have students complete the activities in Handout 1.9.

Handout **1.9**

R-Controlled Vowels (er, ir, ur), Less Common R-Controlled Vowels, and L-Controlled Vowels

Reminder

Er, ir, ur, and sometimes *ear* have the sound /ûr/, as in *her, girl, fur,* and *heard.*

Activities

1. Read the words below:

bird	curl	her	pearl	girl
fern	church	heard	chirp	blur
purse	tern	churn	learn	stern
germ	earn	birth	search	skirt

2. Write the words above in the corresponding columns below:

er	ir	ur	ear
her	bird	curl	pearl
fern	girl	church	heard
tern	chirp	blur	learn
stern	birth	purse	earn
germ	skirt	churn	search

3. Write 3 sentences containing at least 2 /ûr/ words:

   a. Ex: The girls were all in first grade.

   b. Ex: Put the ferns in front of the church.

   c. Ex: We heard the birds chirping outside.

Lesson 1.10 Vowel Digraphs (ai, ay, ee, oa)

Opening

Today we're going to talk about words that contain vowel digraphs. Who remembers what vowel digraphs are? (two adjacent vowels in a syllable pronounced as a single sound) We will divide digraph patterns into two sets: (1) those that are fairly consistently linked to a single sound and (2) those that may have either of two pronunciations. Today we will work on the most common vowel digraphs—those with only one sound.

Objective

Students will read and spell numerous words containing common vowel digraphs.

Procedure

Review the single-sound digraphs on the letter-sound correspondence chart (see Table O.2). List the following digraphs on the board, **review** the sound for each list, and have students **read** the words:

ai	ay*	ee	oa
plain	say	meet	boat
maid	stay	speech	coast
pain	pray	beef	hoax
pail	gray	teeth	soak
waist	sway	steel	groan
train	spray	bleed	cloak
strain	tray	sweep	throat
Spain	stray	street	goal

*The letters *y* and *w* serve as semivowels when they follow another vowel to form a vowel digraph.

NOTE: Have students point out where the vowel digraph comes in a word. Note that *ai, ee,* and *oa* usually come in the middle of words, while *ay* usually comes at the end.

See if students can generate additional words for each list.

Ask students to **spell** the following words from dictation:

pail	goal	meet	boat
beef	tray	waist	sway

Have students **spell** the following sentences as you dictate them:

- Sail your boat at a safe speed.
- The queen groaned as she put on her gray cloak.

Closing

- **What category of letter-sound correspondences did we work on today?** (*vowel digraphs*)
- **Name the four patterns that we discussed.** (ai, ay, ee, *and* oa)

Follow-Up

- Have students complete the activities in Handout 1.10.

Handout

1.10 Vowel Digraphs (ai, ay, ee, oa)

Reminders

Ai, ay, ee, and *oa* are vowel digraphs. Each usually has the long vowel sound of the first letter (this is not the case for all vowel digraphs).

Activities

1. Do we use *ai* or *ay* to spell /ā/ in the middle of words? ai
2. Do we use *ai* or *ay* to spell /ā/ at the end of words? ay
3. Add *ai, ay, ee,* or *oa* to make real words below:

c oa st	w ai st	sp ee ch	spr ay
dism ay	bl ee d	s oa k	str ai n
thr oa t	st ay	t ee th	pl ai n
s ai l	h oa x	t oa st	pl ay

4. Use words above to complete each sentence:

a. I like to sail on the coast.

b. He had to stop his speech because of a sore throat.

c. Make white toast and soak it in milk.

d. Stay late to see the play.

Lesson

1.11 Vowel Digraphs (*oi, oy, au, aw, ew, ue*)

Opening

In the previous lesson, we learned four vowel digraphs. Who remembers what a vowel digraph is? (*two adjacent vowels in a single syllable pronounced as a single sound*) **Today we will study six new vowel digraphs.**

Objective

Students will read and spell words containing vowel digraphs *oi, oy, au, aw, ew* and *ue*.

Procedure

List the following digraphs on the board. Review the sound for each list, and have students **read** the words. See if students can **generate** other words to place in the lists.

oi	oy	au	aw	ew*	ue*
boil	boy	haul	law	few	due
coin	toy	Paul	lawn	grew	glue
toil	Roy	laud	fawn	stew	clue
spoil	coy	cause	dawn	new	blue
point	Troy	vault	straw	flew	cue
moist	joy	daunt	squaw	drew	true
foil	enjoy	fault	shawl	blew	sue

*The vowel digraphs *ew* and *ue* have both /ū/ and /o͞o/ sounds. However, these sounds are rarely confused by students, as /o͞o/ is a variation of /ū/. In addition, *eu* is a less common pattern saying /ū/, as in *feud, feudal, neuter, neutral, neuron, neurotic*, and *neutron*, all words of Greek origin.

Have students **spell** the following sentences as you dictate them:

- The boy had a hawk with sharp claws.
- He blew on the stew and enjoyed his lunch.

Ask students to **identify** where the patterns usually appear in the word. Note that *oi* comes in the middle, while *oy* comes at the end; *au* usually comes in the middle, while *aw* comes at the end or middle before *l* and *n*; *ew* and *ue* both appear at the end of words.

NOTE: Upper grade teachers may include longer words in these lists (e.g., *explain, restrain, pauper, applause, boundary, mildew, nephew, continue*).

Dictate a number of the words presented above. Have students listen for the vowel sound and determine which vowel digraph to use as they **spell** the words on paper.

Closing

- **What did we study today?** (*vowel digraphs*)
- **How many pronunciations can each vowel digraph have?** (*one primary sound*)
- **What did we do with the new vowel digraphs?** (*read lists; contrasted vowel digraphs; generated additional words; spelled words*)

Follow-Up

- Have students write words from the board in their notebooks and find additional words for each pattern in their literature and textbooks.
- Have students complete the activities in Handout 1.11.

Handout
1.11 Vowel Digraphs (oi, oy, au, aw, ew, ue)

Reminders

Some vowel digraphs have two spellings for the same sound. These include *ai* and *ay* spelling the sound /ā/; *oi* and *oy*, /oy/; *au* and *aw*, /aw/; and *ew* and *ue*, /ū/ or /o͞o/.

Activities

1. Write in the blank whether the vowel digraph usually comes in the middle or at the end of words:
   a. *Oi* usually comes in the ___middle___ of words.
   b. *Oy* usually comes at the ___end___ of words.
   c. *Aw* usually comes at the ___end___ of words or at the ___middle___ of words before ___l___ and ___n___.
   d. *Au* usually comes in the ___middle___ of words.
   e. *Ew* usually comes at the ___end___ of words.
   f. *Ue* usually comes at the ___end___ of words.
2. Add *oi, oy, au, aw, ew,* or *ue* to make real words below:

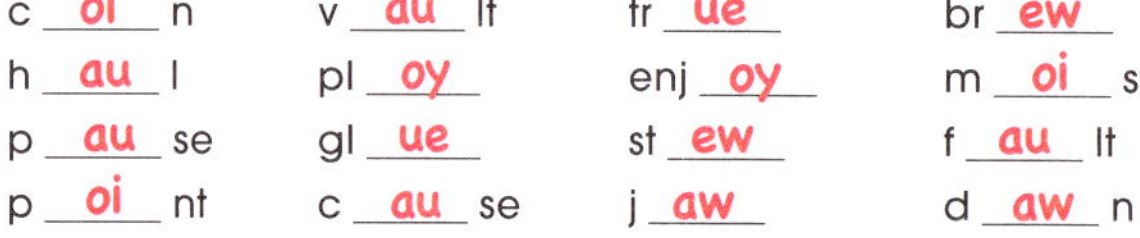

c ___oi___ n	v ___au___ lt	tr ___ue___	br ___ew___
h ___au___ l	pl ___oy___	enj ___oy___	m ___oi___ st
p ___au___ se	gl ___ue___	st ___ew___	f ___au___ lt
p ___oi___ nt	c ___au___ se	j ___aw___	d ___aw___ n

3. Use words above to complete each sentence:
   a. Put the gold ___coin___ in the ___vault___.
   b. ___Haul___ the cart through the ___moist___ yard.
   c. I ___enjoy___ ___true___ stories.

Lesson 1.12 Vowel Digraphs With Two Possible Sounds (oo, ou, ow)

Opening

Today we'll continue to work on vowel digraphs. This time, we'll consider vowel digraphs that may have either of two pronunciations.

Review the two-sound digraphs on the letter-sound correspondence chart (see Table O.2).

Objective

Students will read and spell words containing *oo, ou,* and *ow.*

Procedure

List the following digraphs and their two sounds on the board. Have students **read** the words for each pattern. Ask students to **generate** words to add to each list.

oo		ou		ow	
/o͞o/	**/o͝o/**	**/ou/**	**/ō/***	**/ou/**	**/ō/**
moon	book	out	four	plow	snow
spoon	cook	bout	pour	downtown	blow
broom	shook	shout	court	brown	stow
food	good	pound	course	clown	show
proof	hook	house	soul	frown	throw
booth	stood	proud	mourn	growl	grow
choose	foot	trout	source	crown	flow
stool	look	ground		prowl	slow

*The *ou* spelling long /ō/ is very rare. The *oo* spelling as in *stood* and *book* usually comes before *d* or *k*.

Students will read words and generate additional words if possible. Have students note that *oo* usually occurs in the middle of words, *ou* in the middle, and *ow* at the end, or preceding *l* and *n.*

Have students listen for the vowel sound and determine the appropriate vowel digraph to use as they **spell** the following words:

loon	shout	crown	throw
stoop	court	pouch	prowl
sound	brook	grow	ground

Ask students to **spell** the following sentences as you dictate them:

- Throw the brown book on the footstool.
- The clown frowned at the slow cook.

Closing

- **What did we study today?** (*new vowel digraphs*)
- **How many sounds did each have?** (*two distinct sounds*)
- **What activities did we do?** (*read words; contrasted vowel digraphs; generated new words; spelled words and sentences*)

Follow-Up

- Have students write words from the board in their notebooks and find additional words for each pattern. Or, ask students to look for words with vowel digraphs in their social studies textbook or in a student newspaper.
- Have students complete the activities in Handout 1.12.

Handout

1.12 Vowel Digraphs With Two Possible Sounds (*oo, ou, ow*)

Reminder

Some vowel graphs have two possible pronunciations: *oo*, *ou*, and *ow*.

Activities

1. Fill in the blanks:

   a. The *oo* in __Ex: moon__ sounds like /o͞o/.

   b. The *oo* in __Ex: book__ sounds like /o͝o/.

   c. The *ou* in __Ex: south__ sounds like /ou/.

   d. The *ou* in __Ex: shoulder__ sounds like /ō/.

   e. The *ow* in __Ex: cow__ sounds like /ou/.

   f. The *ow* in __Ex: snow__ sounds like /ō/.

2. Add *oo, ou,* or *ow* to make real words below:

cl _ow_ n	f _ou_ nd	l _oo_ n	sp _oo_ l
sl _ow_	br _oo_ k	p _ou_ ch	b _oo_ th
m _ou_ th	pr _ow_ l	f _ou_ r	st _oo_ d
gr _ow_ l	sh _oo_ k	thr _ow_	p _ou_ r

3. Use some of the words above to complete each sentence:

   a. __Throw__ the fish back in the __brook__.

   b. The __clown__ had a big red __mouth__.

   c. The __loon__ __stood__ near its nest.

Lesson 1.13 Vowel Digraphs With Two Possible Sounds (*ea, ie, ei*)

Opening

Today we'll continue to work on vowel digraphs. This time we'll consider other vowel digraphs that may have either of two pronunciations.

Objective

Students will read and spell words containing *ea, ie,* and *ei.*

Procedure

List the following digraphs and their two sounds on the board. Have students **read** the words for each pattern. Ask students to **generate** words to add to each list.

ea		**ie**		**ei***	
/ē/	**/ĕ/**	**/ē/**	**/ī/**	**/ē/**	**/ā/**
steal	head	thief	die	sheik	vein
meat	dead	chief	tie	seize	veil
team	death	field	lie	either	skein
stream	sweat	shield	pie	neither	reign
heal	health	yield	fie	conceit	eigh (*as in eight, sleigh, weigh, weight, neighbor*)
least	bread	piece		ceiling	
dream	dread	grieve		receive	
sneak	thread	brief		receipt	
mean	meant	priest			

*Teachers may want to consider *ei* words in a separate lesson, especially for younger students.

Ask students to identify where the patterns usually appear in the word. Note that *ea* usually comes in the middle, *ie* as /ē/ in the middle and *ie* as /ī/ at the end of words, and *ei* comes in the middle. Note that after *c,* we use *ei,* not *ea* or *ie.*

Dictate a number of the words presented above for students to **spell**. Have students listen for the vowel sound and determine which vowel digraph to use.

Closing

- **What did we study today?** (*vowel digraphs* ea, ie, *and* ei)
- **How many pronunciations did these vowel digraphs have?** (*two*)
- **What activities did we do?** (*read word lists; contrasted vowel digraphs; generated new words; spelled words*)

Follow-Up

- Have students write words from the board in their notebooks and find additional words for each pattern.
- Have students complete the activities in Handout 1.13.

Handout
1.13 Vowel Digraphs With Two Possible Sounds (*ea, ie, ei*)

Reminders

Ea, *ie*, and *ei* have two possible pronunciations.

Eigh is pronounced like /ā/ in a few words.

Activities

1. Pronunciation:
   a. Which can be pronounced as /ē/ or /ĕ/: *ea*, *ie*, or *ei*? ea
   b. Which can be pronounced as /ī/ or /ē/: *ea*, *ie*, or *ei*? ie
   c. Which can be pronounced as /ē/ or /ā/: *ea*, *ie*, or *ei*? ei

2. Add *ea, ie,* or *ei* (or *eigh*) to make real words below:

sh _ei_ k	sw _ea_ t	st _ea_ l	wh _ea_ t
d _ie_	v _ei_ n	thr _ea_ d	rec _ei_ ve
sn _ea_ k	gr _ie_ ve	l _ie_	n _eigh_ bor
m _ea_ n	m _ea_ nt	th _ie_ f	t _ea_ se

3. Use words above to make complete sentences:
   a. The _sheik_ will _sweat_ in the hot desert.
   b. Will you _receive_ the _wheat_ from the farmer?
   c. The _thief_ will _steal_ his _neighbor_'s bike.

Lesson

1.14 Review of Letter-Sound Correspondences

Opening

Today we will review what we have learned about letter-sound correspondences. We will see if we can define some of the words that are useful for talking about decoding and spelling. We will also see if we can place common patterns on our letter-sound correspondence chart.

Objective

Students will define terms useful for talking about decoding and spelling and place common patterns on the letter-sound correspondence matrix.

Procedure

Have the letter-sound correspondence framework (see Table 1.1) on the board or on a chart, without examples. Ask students to **define** each category and give at least one example.

Write the patterns on the board, and ask students to tell in which cell each pattern should be placed. For example, write *th, bl, oi, nt, ar, g, ee, sl,* and *a* and see if students can **identify** them as consonant digraph, consonant blend, vowel digraph, consonant blend, *r*-controlled vowel, single consonant, vowel digraph, consonant blend, and single vowel, respectively.

Closing

- Check to see if students have any questions regarding the organization of phonics instruction.

Follow-Up

- Have students complete the activities in Handout 1.14.
- Ask students to review the previous lessons and handouts to prepare for the Unit Quiz.
- Administer the Unit 1 Quiz found on the CD.

Handout 1.14 Review of Letter-Sound Correspondences

Reminders

You have now completed the lessons and handouts for Unit 1: Letter-Sound Correspondences. Congratulations! This review handout will help prepare you for your Unit Quiz.

Be sure you know how to identify consonants and vowels, consonant blends, consonant digraphs, and vowel digraphs. You will be asked to circle the short and long vowels in words, along with the consonant blends, consonant digraphs, and vowel digraphs.

Activities

1. Write 5 words that contain consonant blends, but no consonant digraphs:

Ex: trap ___ Ex: grasp ___ Ex: ground ___ Ex: blimp ___ Ex: print

2. Write 5 words that contain consonant digraphs, but no consonant blends:

Ex: chat ___ Ex: which ___ Ex: those ___ Ex: shin ___ Ex: chick

3. Write 5 words that contain vowel digraphs:

Ex: coil ___ Ex: fawn ___ Ex: green ___ Ex: balloon ___ Ex: thread

4. Circle any soft *c* sounds you find in the following words:

clump	(c)ell	i(c)e	(c)ent
(c)ity	spi(c)e	spa(c)e	case

5. Circle any soft *g* sounds you find in the following words:

(g)erms	grave	(g)ym	plun(g)e
(g)ypsy	a(g)e	stran(g)e	plug

Unit

2 Syllable Patterns

Lessons

2.1 Introduction to Syllable Patterns

2.2 Six Syllable Types

2.3 Syllable Division (VC/CV)

2.4 Syllable Division (V/CV)

2.5 Syllable Division (VC/V)

2.6 Syllable Division (Optional VCV)

2.7 Syllable Division (Consonant-*le*)

2.8 Syllable Division (Unstable Digraphs)

2.9 Syllable Division (Adjacent Vowels)

2.10 Review of Syllable Patterns

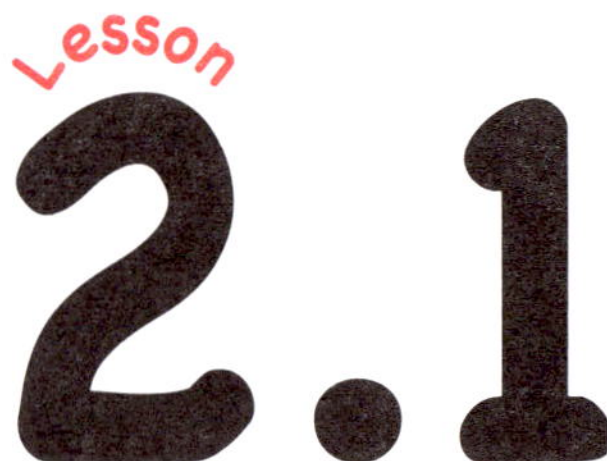

Introduction to Syllable Patterns

This unit deals with syllable patterns. In the next few lessons, we will learn about six different syllable types and practice dividing long words into syllables as we read and spell unfamiliar words. When you learn to divide words into syllables, you can break long words into smaller parts.

Objective

Students will learn the six syllable types and strategies for syllable division.

Procedure

Who knows what a syllable is? Write *syllable* on the board.

Probe to get a definition close to this: (a unit of sequential speech sounds containing a vowel and consonants (if any) preceding or following that vowel, such as /ĭ/, /dĭ/, /ĭd/, and /dĭd/). Say several multisyllabic words. Begin with the names of students in your class. Have students repeat the name, say the name in syllables, and count the syllables. Students may find it useful to clap out each syllable. Then add other words of two to five syllables, such as those below:

Sam (1)	Angela (3)
Carlos (2)	Elizabeth (4)
vacation (3)	story (2)
population (4)	artichoke (3)
independent (4)	reincarnation (5)
degeneration (5)	reconstructionist (5)
multisensory (5)	cucumber (3)

Dividing words into syllables provides new strategies for reading and spelling longer, unfamiliar words. By dividing words into syllables, we don't need to be able to read or spell the entire long word. We can break the word into parts and then put the parts back together. We will have a lot of practice working with longer words in this unit.

There are some important points you should know about syllables. Each syllable must have a vowel sound. Sometimes that sound is made up of two vowels in a vowel digraph. Always look for the vowels in a word. If there is a consonant between the vowels, you probably have more than one syllable.

NOTE: This is not the case in final vowel-consonant-*e* (VC*e*) patterns, as in *like, made, cope,* or *cute,* where the final *e* is always silent.

Sometimes it is useful to pick out which syllable in a word gets the accent, or stress. When you look up words in the dictionary, the bold apostrophe (i.e., ') tells you the accented syllable. Sometimes more than one syllable in a long word gets the stress.

Pronounce the following words and ask, **Can you tell which syllable gets the primary accent in the following words?**

o'/pen	be/gin'	pre/dic'/tion
tar'/get	mar'/ket	in/for/ma'/tion
trans'/fer	pre/dict'	va/ca'/tion
ten'/nis	nap'/kin	ap/pro'/pri/ate

Ask students to repeat the words after you, listening for accented syllables.

NOTE: Some children have great difficulty hearing accent, no matter how long you emphasize this.

Closing

- **What did we study today?** (*the concept of syllable*)
- **Why is it useful to isolate syllables when you read and spell?** (*breaks words down into smaller units*)
- Tell students they will be learning about specific syllable types and syllable division patterns in the coming lessons.

Follow-Up

- Have students complete the activities in Handout 2.1.

Handout
2.1 Introduction to Syllable Patterns

Reminders

A syllable is a unit of sequential speech sounds containing a vowel and consonants (if any) that precede or follow that vowel (e.g., /ĭ/, /pĭ/, /ĭp/, /pĭp/).

Every syllable contains at least one vowel.

Activities

1. Count the vowels in the following words, then read each word either aloud or silently. (Remember that the silent final *e* doesn't count as a separate vowel, so don't include it in your count.)

Ex: catnip 2	muffin 2	Beth 1	bunny 2
fund 1	library 3	lamppost 2	department 3
identical 4	revitalize 4	president 3	conducted 3
executive 4	proposal 3	public 2	September 3

2. Use some of the words above to complete these sentences:

a. Jane and Sally were identical twins.

b. My birthday is in September.

c. The leader conducted the high school band.

d. The vice president liked the blueberry muffin.

Lesson

2.2 Six Syllable Types

Opening

Once you know the six syllable types and the major patterns for syllable division, you will be able to read many multisyllabic words. There are six distinct syllable types: (1) closed, (2) open, (3) vowel-consonant-*e*, (4) vowel team or vowel digraph, (5) consonant-*le*, and (6) *r*-controlled. Closed and open syllables account for almost 75% of English syllables.

Objective

Students will learn the six syllable types and read and spell words containing each type of syllable.

Procedure

Closed Syllables

Each closed syllable ends in one or more consonants with a vowel preceding the consonants. A closed syllable may be represented by VC (*at*), VCC (*egg*), VCCC (*etch*), CVC (*mat*), CVCC (*fast*), CCVC (*spin*), CCVCC (*blimp*), CCVCCC (*grudge*), CCCVC (*split*), CCCVCC (*sprint*), or CCCVCCC (*scratch*). The vowel will have its short sound (˘). Read these closed-syllable words. Write the following words on the board or in a flip chart.

at	ant	itch	ditch
map	blast	fetch	quick
stench	clock	trot	hunt
blimp	match	crib	splash
Dutch	bridge	belt	bunk

Ask students to **spell** some of the words listed above or other closed-syllable words.

Open Syllables

An open syllable contains a vowel at the end of the syllable (CV), and the vowel usually has its long sound (¯). Read the following words that contain open syllables. Write the following words on the board.

hi	sky	my	go
me	she	we	shy

Vowel-Consonant-*e* Syllable (VC*e*)

Read these words. Notice the final silent *e* marks the vowel as long. Write the following words on the board.

made	time	vote	cute
Pete	place	sprite	mute
crave	June	wrote	pride
plume	choke	crude	grime

Spell the following words as I dictate them to you. Read some of the words from the list above aloud for students to **spell**.

Vowel Digraph Syllable

Read these one-syllable words containing a vowel digraph. Write the following words on the board.

steam	boat	strew	bait
spray	bread	breed	gown
joint	flown	toast	Spain
Paul	sweep	round	fawn

Now, *spell* these words as I dictate them to you. Read some of the words above aloud to students for them to **spell**.

Consonant-*le* Syllable

A consonant-*le* syllable usually starts with a consonant that is part of that syllable. For example, *table* has a long *a* because *ble* stays together, making the first syllable in the word an open syllable, t\ā. In contrast, *crumble* contains *crum* and *ble*, with *crum* being a closed syllable.

Read the following two-syllable words and identify the consonant-*le* syllable, as well as the sound of the preceding vowel. Write the following words on the board.

table	crumble	fumble	thimble
cradle	cuddle	brittle	kettle
poodle	nimble	raffle	smuggle
sniffle	puzzle	bible	bugle

Now, spell these words as I dictate them to you. Read some of the words from the list above aloud for students to **spell**.

R-Controlled Syllables

These syllables contain one of the *r*-controlled patterns we studied in Unit 1, which contain a vowel just before the *r*.

Read the following words and identify the *r*-controlled pattern. Write the following words on the board.

park	stork	bear	church
snarl	heard	hurt	storm
porch	marsh	stern	shirt
birch	sport	sharp	twirl

Spell these words as I dictate them to you. Read some of the words from the list above aloud to students for them to **spell**.

Closing

- **What did we study today?** *(the six syllable types)*
- **Why is it important to know these syllable types?** (*they will be helpful as we begin to read and spell longer, polysyllabic words*)

Follow-Up

Have students complete the activities in Handout 2.2.

Handout

2.2 Six Syllable Types

Reminders

Closed syllables—VC pattern; have a short vowel; a consonant directly follows the short vowel (e.g., *at, mat, plan, chimp, sprint*)

Open syllables—CV pattern; have a long vowel; the vowel is at the end of a syllable (e.g., *go, baby, bonus, oboe, begin, label*)

Vowel-consonant-*e*—VC-*e* pattern;syllables end with a silent *e*, making the preceding vowel long (e.g., *blame, smoke, smile, mute, Pete*).

Vowel team syllables—Sometimes called *vowel digraph syllables;* contain two adjacent vowels in the same syllable (e.g., *brain, coast, peach, coil, cause*).

Consonant-*le* syllables—Place the consonant with the -*le* in a syllable (e.g., *bugle, tumble, puzzle, turtle, purple*).

***R*-controlled syllables—**Contain a vowel just before the *r* (e.g., *farm, turn, chirp, berm, horn*).

Activities

1. Underline the words that contain closed syllables:

Ex: flat	spin	punch
mate	fetch	sprout
she	clock	sprint

2. Underline the words with open syllables:

Ex: she	flash	try
fly	team	cry
we	blimp	go

3. Underline the words with vowel-consonant-*e* syllables:

Ex: plate	split	slide
grip	vote	fly
spoke	crime	smash

4. Underline the words containing vowel digraphs:

Ex: steam	sleep	Paul
crash	church	coin
flout	thief	fawn

5. Underline the words with consonant-*le* syllables:

Ex: bugle	simple	puzzle
final	table	bubble
turtle	slide	smile

6. Underline the words with *r*-controlled syllables:

Ex: part	fern	church
runt	girl	search
thirst	curl	twist

7. Write 3 sentences using at least 3 syllable types (i.e., closed, open, vowel-consonant-*e*, consonant-*le*, *r*-controlled) in each sentence. Ex: My friend has a turtle. (*open, vowel digraph, consonant*-le)

Ex: a. The girl twisted her braids. ____.

b. His ____

____.

c. Five ____

____.

Syllable Division (VC/CV)

Opening

Today we will work on the closed type of syllable and see what happens with two- and three-syllable words containing closed syllables.

Objective

Students will read and then spell many words containing the VCCV pattern.

Procedure

Write the word *rabbit* on the board. Point out the VCCV (vowel-consonant-consonant-vowel) pattern and label it.

r **a b b i** t
VCCV

Ask students where the word is divided (*rab/bit*). (Or, remind students that words are usually divided between two consonants: VC/CV.)

Show the first syllable, *rab,* and ask if the vowel is short or long. Remind students that a vowel followed by a consonant in the same syllable is almost always short (just like in the one-syllable words we studied earlier). Show them the short vowel marking (˘). This is called a *breve.*

Tell students that the consonant does not need to be an identical consonant. Write the word *napkin* on the board. Point out the VCCV pattern and label it.

n **a p k i** n
VCCV

Ask students where the word is divided (*nap/kin*).

Have students tell you where to divide the following words as you read each aloud. Then write the words on the board and ask students to **read** the words.

tennis	campus	velvet	muffin
candid	pastel	funnel	unfit
muslin	fossil	bandit	optic
bobbin	nutmeg	goblin	cutlet

NOTE: You might also ask students to mark the short vowel with the breve (˘).

If you choose, have students tell you where to divide the following three-syllable words fitting the VCCV pattern. Then have students **read** the words as you write them on the board, concentrating on the syllable patterns to help them with vowel sounds.

carpenter	masterly	tenderness	infantile
peppermint	badminton	flabbergast	blunderbuss
organdy	fantastic	Wisconsin	September
misfortune	bombastic	alfalfa	hobgoblin

Dictate the following VCCV words to students for them to **spell**. Remind students of the pattern. (Be sure students repeat the word, listen for syllables, write, and then check their spelling as you write the word on the board.)

velvet	humbug	magnet	cactus
tandem	convex	goblet	poplin
catnip	combat	mandate	alcove
fantastic	distemper	Atlantic	flabbergast

Closing

- **What kind of words did we read and spell today?** (*two- and three-syllable words with a VCCV syllable pattern*)
- **Is the first vowel long or short in VCCV words?** (*short*)
- **What did we do with our words today?** (*divided words into syllables; counted syllables; read and spelled multisyllabic words*)

Follow-Up

- Look for words containing the VCCV pattern in a classroom reading selection.
- Have students complete the activities in Handout 2.3.

Handout

2.3 Syllable Division (VC/CV)

Reminders

When a VCCV pattern occurs in a word, we usually divide between the two consonants. For example, *rabbit* is divided as *rab/bit*, and *napkin* is divided as *nap/kin*.

Closed syllables may be represented by VC (*at*), VCC (*egg*), VCCC (*etch*), CVC (*mat*), CVCC (*fast*), CCVC (*spin*), CCVCC (*blimp*), CCVCCC (*grudge*), CCCVC (*split*), CCCVCC (*sprint*), and CCCVCCC (*scratch*).

NOTE: Some VCCV words contain *r*-controlled vowels, such as in *tar/get*, *mer/ger*, and *bar/ker*.

Activities

1. Divide the following VCCV words into syllables. Mark the vowel in the first syllable with a breve (˘) if it is short. In three-syllable words, mark the first two vowels if they are short. Read each word to yourself.

Ex: mĕm/ber	sĕc|tor	păs|tel	mĭt|ten
tĕn|nis	cŭt|let	căm|pus	vĭc|tim
mĕn|tal	lămp|post	car|pet	hŏb|gŏb|lin
Wĭs|cŏn|sin	dĭs|tĕm|per	făn|tăs|tic	Ăt|lăn|tic

2. Use some of the words above to write complete sentences:

Ex: a. We played tennis on the Wisconsin campus.

b. ______________________________.

c. ______________________________.

Syllable Division (V/CV)

Opening

Today we'll work on a new possibility for syllable division. When one consonant stands between two vowels (VCV), the first vowel is usually long, as the consonant usually goes with the second syllable (V/CV). This long vowel syllable is called an *open syllable.* A long vowel is marked by a macron (¯) in the dictionary.

Objective

Students will read and spell two-syllable words having the V/CV pattern.

Procedure

Show the following examples:

VCV
locust (lō/cust)
tripod (trī/pod)
rival (rī/val)
caper (cā/per)

Remind students the vowel is long when it comes at the end of a syllable.

Write the following words on the board. Have students divide them into syllables based on the V/CV pattern of syllable division they just learned, and then ask them to read the words. You may mark the long vowels with a macron.

pagan	spoken	tulip	human
craven	rodent	final	topaz
tirade	vacate	label	unit
sequel	vocal	totem	music

I will dictate a number of two-syllable words for you to *spell.* Say the word after me, write the word, and check it as I write the word on the board. Remind students that a single vowel will make the long sound.

shiny	pilot	zero
silent	focus	tirade
hobo	lazy	sofa

Closing

- **What kinds of words did we study today?** (*two-syllable words with a V/CV syllable pattern*)
- **Is the vowel at the end of the first syllable long or short?** (*long*)
- **Is a syllable that ends in a vowel open or closed?** (*open*)

Follow-Up

- Have students find words that fit the two syllable patterns studied so far (i.e., VC/CV and V/CV).
- Have students complete the activities in Handout 2.4.

Handout 2.4 Syllable Division (V/CV)

Reminder

When one consonant stands between two vowels (VCV), we usually divide after the first vowel, making an open syllable with a long vowel sound.

Activities

1. Divide the following words into syllables. Mark the long vowel with a macron (¯) in the first syllable. Read the words to yourself.

Ex: lī/lac	ō/pen	bē/gin	rē/mote
dē/light	pī/lot	hō/bo	prō/mote
mō/ment	pō/ny	grā/vy	zē/ro
bā/con	spī/cy	cō/ma	cū/pid

2. Use words above to complete each sentence:

a. ___Open___ the barn door for the small ___pony___.

b. The airline ___pilot___ turned on his ___remote___ control.

c. I like brown ___gravy___ on my mashed potatoes.

d. The ___bacon___ will be done cooking in a ___moment___.

Lesson

2.5 Syllable Division (VC/V)

Opening

Today we'll work on an alternative division for the VCV syllable pattern. Sometimes the vowel is short, like when it is followed by a consonant in the first syllable (VC/V). Remember that the short vowel syllable is called a *closed syllable.* When you see a VCV word, first try to divide it after the first vowel. If the word doesn't make sense, divide it after the consonant.

Objective

Students will read and spell two-syllable words with the VC/V pattern.

Procedure

Show the following examples:

	VCV
solid	(sŏl/id)
cabin	(căb/in)
seven	(sĕv/en)
limit	(lĭm/it)

Remind students that the vowel is short when it is followed by a consonant at the end of a syllable.

Write the following words on the board. Have students divide them into syllables based on the VC/V pattern of syllable division they just learned, and then ask them to read the words. Mark the first vowel with the breve (˘).

solid	seven	legend	rigid
cabin	tepid	closet	colic
banish	limit	habit	tragic
gravel	talent	panel	camel

How do these words differ from the words in Lesson 2.4? (*those words divided after the vowel, but these divide after the consonant*)

I will dictate a number of words for you to *spell.* Say the word after me, write the word, read it over, and check it as I write the word on the board. Remind students that these words will not have a double consonant.

static	travel	gravel	camel
habit	banish	limit	comic

Closing

- **What kinds of words did we study today?** (*two-syllable words with a VC/V pattern*)
- **Is the first vowel long or short?** (*short*)
- **Is a syllable that ends in a consonant open or closed?** (*closed*)

Follow-Up

- Have students find words in books that fit the three syllable patterns studied so far (i.e., VC/CV, V/CV, and VC/V).
- Have students complete the activities in Handout 2.5.

Handout 2.5 Syllable Division (VC/V)

Reminder

When you see a VCV pattern in an unfamiliar word, first try to divide after the first vowel, as we did in the previous lesson. If the word doesn't make sense, try to divide after the consonant, and you will have a closed syllable with a short vowel.

Activities

1. Divide the following words into syllables after the consonant. Mark the first vowel with the breve (˘). Read the words to yourself.

Ex: lĕv/el	hăb/it	văn/ish	lĭm/it
frŏl/ic	vĭs/it	plăn/et	căb/in
prŏp/er	frĭg/id	căv/ern	fĭn/ish
băn/ish	sĕv/en	trăv/el	tŏp/ic

2. Use some of the words above to write complete sentences:

Ex: a. The seven students will travel together after they finish school

______________________________.

b. ______________________________

______________________________.

c. ______________________________

______________________________.

d. ______________________________

______________________________.

Syllable Division (Optional VCV)

Opening

Today we will review the two ways to divide words having the VCV pattern. As you divide and read words, remember to first separate the word after the first vowel (V/CV); this will give you an open syllable with a long vowel. (Usually the consonant goes in the next syllable.) If the word makes no sense when pronounced that way, then divide after the consonant (VC/V); this will give you a closed syllable with a short vowel.

Objective

Students will review words containing VCV syllables. They will read and spell words and determine whether to divide after the first vowel or after the consonant.

Procedure

Write the following words on the board. Have students **divide** the following words into syllables and **read** the words:

tulip	river	omit	moment
gravy	tuna	total	lilac
model	timid	hoping	finish
baby	human	spiral	famish

Spell **the following words that I dictate:**

pony	emit	virus	cabin
limit	humid	silent	gravel

Closing

- **What did we do today?** (*reviewed V/CV and VC/V rules for syllable division; divided, read, and spelled words*)
- **If you don't know how to divide a word into syllables, which strategy do you try first?** (*V/CV*)

Follow-Up

- Ask students to find VCV words in their science textbook. Have students, working in pairs, divide and read the words to their classmates. Remind students to try the long sound (V/CV) first, as this is the most frequently found VCV pattern.
- Have students complete the activities in Handout 2.6.

Handout
2.6 Syllable Division (Optional VCV)

Reminder

If you see a VCV pattern in an unfamiliar word, try dividing after the first vowel (V/CV); this will give you an open syllable with a long vowel. If the word doesn't make sense when pronounced this way, divide after the consonant (VC/V); this will give you a closed syllable with a short vowel.

Activities

1. Divide the words below into syllables. Then mark the first vowel with a macron if it's long or a breve if it's short.

Ex: trăv/el	pī/lot	mū/sic	lĭm/it
nŏv/el	hăb/it	pā/per	sī/lent
văn/ish	clō/ver	săt/in	pŭn/ish
hō/tel	cā/per	căb/in	fē/ver

2. Use some of the words above to complete these sentences:

a. The pilot likes to travel from state to state.

b. He won't drive over the speed limit.

c. People who live on islands may get cabin fever.

d. The fancy hotel had satin bedspreads.

Syllable Division (Consonant-*le*)

Opening

Many two-syllable words end in *le,* preceded by a consonant. The consonant always goes with the *le* to make up a syllable. We'll be reading and writing many words with this consonant-*le* (C-*le*) pattern.

Objective

Students will identify, read, and spell words containing the C-*le* type of syllable.

Procedure

The C-*le* syllable always appears at the end of words. The *e* is always silent and the syllable lacks a vowel sound. The dictionary shows this omission by using an apostrophe to replace the vowel sound (e.g., *can'/d'l*).

Write the most common C-*le* syllables on the board and have students pronounce them:

ple tle fle ble gle cle zle kle

Always divide the words just before the consonant-*le* pattern. For example, *thim/ble* and *sta/ble.* Notice that the first syllable in *thimble* has a short vowel sound because it is a closed syllable and that the first syllable in *stable* has a long vowel sound because it is an open syllable.

Write the following words on the board. Ask students to divide these words into syllables and pronounce the words.

bubble	handle	sprinkle	sniffle
riddle	table	rifle	jiggle
giggle	ruffle	whittle	fizzle
stifle	sample	crumple	throttle
juggle	ankle	puzzle	maple
marble	crackle	shuttle	dwindle
needle	bugle	tremble	muddle

When the consonant before the *le* has an *st* before *it* (*stle*), the *t* is silent. We hear only /s'l/. The division is usually after the *s.* Write the following words on the board. Ask students to divide and read the words.

castle	hustle	thistle	whistle
bustle	jostle	rustle	gristle
nestle	bristle	wrestle	trestle

As students write the following phrases, it is important for them to listen for a short or long vowel sound in the syllable before the C-*le* syllable. Alert students that they will be **spelling** two- to three-word phrases today, not just single words.

maple tree	dense jungle
whittle the sticks	crumple our papers
wooden rifle	large kettle
small poodle	simple class
empty table	church steeple

For upper grades, you may add the following:

feeble answers	lengthy battle
thirty bottles	difficult puzzle
nimble dancers	the middle countries
enormous castle	wrestle your brother

Closing

- **What did we do today?** (*learned about the consonant-le syllable for syllable division; read and spelled words containing C*-le *syllables*)
- **What is important to remember with these syllables?** (*they always appear in the second syllable; three letters, C*-le, *always go together to form the syllable*)

Follow-Up

- Give students a number of words containing C-*le* syllables. Ask them to write a paragraph using the words.
- Have students complete the activities in Handout 2.7.

Handout

2.7 Syllable Division (Consonant-*le*)

UNIT 2

30

Lesson 2.7

79

Reminders

In words ending in consonant-*le*, the consonant always goes in the same syllable as the *le*. The consonant-*le* syllable is usually the final syllable in a two-syllable word.

You will also see *stle* in the final syllable, where the *t* is silent. The division is usually after the *s*, as in *whis/tle*, pronounced *hwis' əl.*

Activities

1. Divide the following words into syllables. Then mark the vowels with a breve if short or a macron if long. Then read the words to yourself. (Some first syllables will be *r*-controlled.)

Ex: thĭm/ble	tā/ble	gĭg/gle	tŭm/ble
thĭs/tle	bŭb/ble	pĭm/ple	pŭz/zle
thĭm/ble	trŭn/dle	thrŏt/tle	sĭm/ple
căt/tle	căn/dle	rī/fle	hŭs/tle
stī/fle	căs/tle	stā/ble	tur/tle
rŭm/ble	ăp/ple	crā/dle	băf/fle

2. Use one of the words above to answer each riddle:

a. Eat me every day to keep the doctor away: apple

b. You keep horses in me: stable

c. You can shoot squirrels with me: rifle

d. I am a kind of bush: thistle

3. Draw a line from a syllable in column 1 to a syllable in column 2 to make a word:

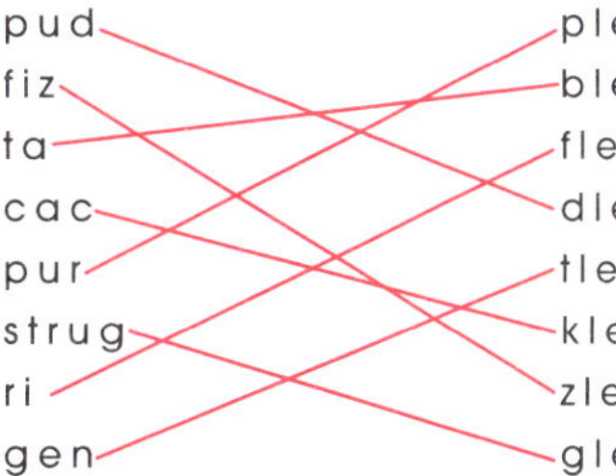

Syllable Division (Unstable Digraphs)

NOTE: The next two lessons may be irrelevant for younger children and may be skipped. The patterns should be pointed out to students in the upper grades, however, as words containing these patterns appear in their literature and content area textbooks. These words are another example of a case where the saying "When two vowels go walking, the first does the talking" (and the second does nothing) causes problems.

Opening

Today we will discuss some surprising words. These words have two vowels together and may look like vowel digraphs, but they are not digraphs, because the vowels occur in different syllables. We divide words between the vowels in this case (CV/VC). We will read and spell a number of these words today. We call these vowel pairs *unstable digraphs.*

Objective

Students will learn about words containing two adjacent vowels where we divide the words between the vowels.

Procedure

Sometimes pairs of vowels well established in the student's mind as vowel digraphs separate into their individual sounds.

NOTE: Some of these separations occur between prefixes and roots.

Write the following headings and words on the board:

a i	e a	e i	e u
mosaic	create	being	museum
archaic	theater	reinforce	nucleus
laity	linear	reinstate	
	permeate	deity	
	preamble		

i e	o a	o e	o i
science	oasis	poem	going
client	Joanne	coerce	egoist
quiet	coagulate	coexist	doing
orient*	boa	poetry	

o o	u e	u i
zoology	duet	fluid
cooperate	duel	fluidity
coordinate	fuel	bruin
	fluent	fruition
	minuet	annuity
	influence	ambiguity

*When *i* comes at the end of a syllable and precedes another vowel, it often says /ē/ (e.g., *radio, stadium, experience, barbarian*).

Please divide the words in the list into syllables and *read* the words.

Next, you're going to practice *spelling* some words. Listen to each syllable as I say the word. Repeat the word aloud. *Write* the words and check your spelling as I write them on the board.

mosaic	quiet	oasis
cruel	poetry	client
museum	science	coordinate

Closing

- **What did we learn today?** (*unstable digraphs occur in words that are divided into syllables between two adjacent vowels*)

Follow-Up

- Have students complete the activities in Handout 2.8.

Handout

2.8 Syllable Division (Unstable Digraphs)

Reminder

A few words have two adjacent vowels that are not vowel digraphs. They look like vowel digraphs, but they are not, because the vowels are in different syllables. In this case, we divide the word between the two vowels.

Activities

1. Divide the words below into syllables and mark each vowel with a macron (¯) if it's long or a breve (˘) if it's short. Some syllables contain vowels with the schwa sound, which will be discussed in Unit 3. If you don't hear a long or short sound, don't mark the vowel. Note that some words have three, four, or five syllables. Divide the entire word into syllables.

Ex: mō/sā/ĭc	bō/a	flū/ent	flū/id
scī/ence	crē/āte	bē/ing	mū/sē/um
per/mē/āte	ē/gō/ist	cō/ēx/ist	cō/ăg/ū/late
pō/ĕt	pō/ĕt/ry	quī/ĕt	clī/ĕnt
zō/ŏl/ō/gy	cō/ŏp/er/āte	mĭn/ū/ĕt	ăm/bĭg/ū/ĭ/ty
fū/el	dū/ĕt	ō/ā/sĭs	ar/chā/ĭc

2. Use words from above to complete each sentence:

a. The ___poet___ read his poems at the ___museum___.

b. I like animals, so I want to study ___zoology___ in college.

c. The cost of ___fuel___ made the ___client___ very nervous.

d. I like to dance the ___minuet___ and to sing a ___duet___ with my friend.

Syllable Division (Adjacent Vowels)

Opening

Today we will discuss another group of interesting words. These words also have two vowels together, but they are not digraphs either. They include *ao, eo, ia, io, iu, ua, uo,* and *uu.* In fact, these adjacent vowels are never digraphs, as they always appear in separate syllables. Again, we divide words between the vowels (CV/VC). We will read and spell a number of these words today.

Objective

Students will divide, read, and spell multisyllabic words containing two adjacent vowels (dividing between the vowels).

Procedure

Write the following headings and words on the board:

a o	e o	i a	i o
chaos	neon	trial	lion
chaotic	peony	friar	riot
aorta	video	diamond	scion
	meteor	dialect	priority
	hideous	diary	iodine
	bounteous	zodiac	violin
	plenteous	denial	violet
	geology	material	champion
	geometry		pioneer

i u	u a	u o	u u
triumph	truant	tenuous	vacuum
medium	nuance	continuous	continuum
stadium	graduate	impetuous	
opium	annual	contiguous	
radium	visual		
	casual		
	virtual		

First, divide the words in each list between the two adjacent vowels. Next, make any other necessary division marks if there are other syllables in the word. Then, read the words aloud.

Next, you're going to practice *spelling* some words. Listen to each syllable as I say the word. Repeat the word aloud. *Write* the word and check your spelling as I write the words on the board.

violin	riot	pioneer
continuum	dialect	diagram
stadium	graduate	continual

Closing

- **What did we learn today?** (*to divide words into syllables containing two adjacent vowels that are not vowel digraphs*)

Follow-Up

- Have students complete the activities in Handout 2.9.

Handout

2.9 Syllable Division (Adjacent Vowels)

Reminder

Some adjacent vowels are never digraphs and will always be divided between the vowels. These include *ao, eo, ia, io, iu, ua, uo,* and *uu.*

The letter *i* is sometimes pronounced /ē/ when it comes at the end of a syllable and before another vowel, as in *stadium* and *studio.*

Activities

1. Divide the words below into syllables. Mark the vowels as long or short if you can.

Ex: chā/ŏs	vĭd|ē|ō	dī|a|lĕct	ī|ō|dīne
vī|ō|lĭn	zō|di|ăc	trī|ŭmph	ĕd|ū|cāte
căs|ū|al	ăn|nū|al	stā|di|ŭm	mē|tē|or
gē|ŏl|ō|gy	dē|nī|al	ma|ter|i|al	chăm|pi|ons
prī|or|ĭ|ty	boun|tē|ous	nē|ŏn	rī|ŏt
dī|a|grăm	rā|di|ŭm	pī|ō|neer	frī|ar

2. Use words from above to complete each sentence:

a. Fans in the football __stadium__ yelled for the new __champions__.

b. Draw a __diagram__ of the cello, viola, and __violin__.

c. The space __pioneer__ made a __video__ of the fiery __meteor__.

d. I enjoy learning about rocks, so I may study __geology__ in the future.

Lesson 2.10 Review of Syllable Patterns

Opening

For the past several decoding lessons, we have studied syllable patterns. Today we are going to review the most frequent patterns, determine where the words are divided, and read and spell multisyllabic words. We will also learn one additional type of pattern (VCCCV).

Objective

Students will review syllable patterns as they divide words into syllables and read them.

Procedure

Here is a list of words for you to divide into syllables. First, you will tell me where to *divide* them. Then, you will *read* the words to me.

NOTE: If you omitted Lessons 2.8 and 2.9, you also should delete words with adjacent vowels in different syllables (i.e., *triumph, radio, poem, premium, pioneer, fluid*).

tumble	triumph	table	radio
puzzle	napkin	hamlet	pilot
giggle	poem	bounty	camel
rabbit	premium	muffin	bugle
cabin	hero	hobgoblin	pioneer
demon	fluid	crumble	concave
campus	hero	travel	bandit

You should be aware that some words have three consonants between two vowels (VCCCV). When this happens, the syllable division usually occurs between a blend or between a consonant digraph and the other single consonant. Where would these words be divided?

inflate	partner	pantry	pumpkin
explode	hundred	embrace	blindness
astronaut	muskmelon	bashful	worship

Closing

- **Why it is useful to learn the different patterns for syllable division?** (*you can break words down into smaller parts in order to read and spell unknown words*)

Follow-Up

- Have students complete the activities in Handout 2.10.
- Administer the Unit 2 Quiz found on the CD.

Handout
2.10 Review of Syllable Patterns

Reminder

You have studied a variety of syllable types and possible ways to divide words into syllables in order to read and spell unfamiliar words.

Activities

1. Divide the following words into syllables using the new strategies you have learned.

Ex: rec/tan/gle	pi|lot	fab|u|lous	ze|ro
con|tin|ue	tri|fle	flat|bed	gin|ger
trav|el	sim|ple	tar|nish	hu|man
vi|rus	mid|dle	viv|id	sub|way
dis|tem|per	pep|per|mint	op|tic	bad|min|ton
sli|my	boun|ty	bob|bin	book|case

2. Draw a line from the syllable in column 1 to the syllable in column 2 to make a word:

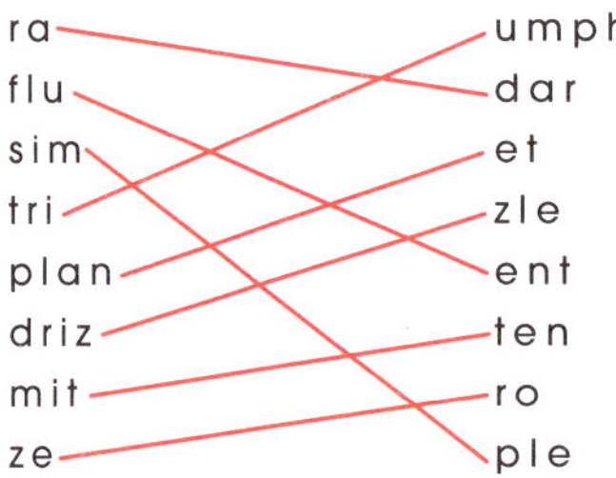

3. Use the following words to fill in the blanks in the sentences below:

visit varnish steeple studio vacant quietly

a. ___Visit___ the ___studio___ to see the new artwork.

b. The church ___steeple___ needs repair.

c. Move ___quietly___ through the ___vacant___ lots.

d. ___Varnish___ the new woodwork to keep it smooth and shiny.

Unit

3 Layers of Language: Anglo-Saxon, Latin, Greek

Lessons

3.1 Introduction to Layers of Language

3.2 Anglo-Saxon Letter-Sound Correspondences and Syllable Patterns

3.3 Anglo-Saxon Morpheme Patterns (Compound Words)

3.4 Anglo-Saxon Morpheme Patterns (Prefixes)

3.5 Anglo-Saxon Morpheme Patterns (Suffixes)

3.6 Anglo-Saxon Non-Phonetic Words

3.7 Summary of the Anglo-Saxon Influence on English

3.8 Latin Letter-Sound Correspondences

3.9 Latin Syllable Patterns

3.10 Latin Morpheme Patterns

3.11 Greek Letter-Sound Correspondences

3.12 Greek Syllable Patterns

3.13 Greek Morpheme Patterns

3.14 Review of Layers of Language

Lesson

3.1 Introduction to Layers of Language

In this unit, we will study how the languages of different countries influenced how English words are written today. English is primarily made up of words of Anglo-Saxon, Latin, and Greek origin. We will learn how English words of Anglo-Saxon origin differ from the Latin- and Greek-based words and how even these two languages have different characteristics. Knowing about these languages will make reading and spelling English words easier.

Opening

Today we will have more of a history lesson than a reading lesson as we learn how written language, and especially written English, grew.

NOTE: For more information on this subject, see the Resources section of this manual.

Objective

Students will learn how the structure and spelling of English words are influenced by word origin, especially words coming to us from the Anglo-Saxon, Latin, and Greek languages.

Procedure

The Growth of Written English

For many centuries, people could only talk to one another about their ideas and feelings. People realized it would be convenient if they could leave lasting messages for one another. As no writing systems or alphabets existed, these ancient people began drawing pictures. They drew pictures on pieces of bark or bone, or even on the walls of caves. Hundreds of these *picture drawings* can be found in India, southern Europe, and South America today. Some are over 75,000 years old.

Some 5,000 years ago, people in Sumerian and Egyptian cultures developed visual symbols in which each symbol, or *pictograph,* stood for a whole word or syllable. Other pictographs include Scandinavian Stone Age and Bronze Age carvings. Later, the American Indians drew pictures as messages and records for their tribesmen. These drawings can be found in New Mexico and Arizona, as well as other places inhabited by Native Americans. In picture writing, a scene represents a story. Ancient Egyptians developed *hieroglyphics,* small pictures used to stand for a word.

Another type of early writing was *ideograms,* often called *logographs.* Chinese scholars invented these simple drawings to represent words that were difficult to draw in picture form. Educated Chinese readers may learn more than 6,000 characters representing 40,000 words.

Because writing with ideograms or hieroglyphics was very slow and because many characters had to be learned, people designed a symbol system almost 3,000 years ago. In this alphabetic system, each symbol stands for a sound. This phonetic writing has been modified into the English alphabetic system we use today.

Show illustrations of picture drawings, pictographs, and ideograms. Children enjoy writing stories using their own symbols. Give students a table with Egyptian hieroglyphics. (See www.kidzone.ws/cultures/egypt/hieroglyph.htm or www.jimloy.com/hiero/yourname.gif.) Have the children write their names in hieroglyphics.

English has been greatly influenced by other languages. It did not originate in England, as you might think. The oldest words came from tribes from northern Europe who invaded England and wiped out the civilization they found there.

These Anglo-Saxon conquerors had few words, mostly those connected with things they used and the actions of their daily lives. This Old English (used from 450 to 1150 C.E. (Common Era)) resembled German. Many of the words we use today came from Anglo-Saxon origin. Most of our short, one-syllable words are Anglo-Saxon, for example, words like *bed, cold, sit, but, milk, field, walk,* and *eat.* The Anglo-Saxon words are common, everyday, down-to-earth words.

Norman invaders came in 1066 C.E., during the Norman Conquest, from what is now France. Their language contained many words they had learned from the Romans, who at one time had conquered France. The language of the Romans was called Latin; we have many words that come from Latin. The period of Middle English began after the Norman-French invasion and continued to about 1500.

Later, scholars in England borrowed words directly from Latin itself, which for centuries was the language of educated men and women all over Europe. Many of our longer and more scholarly words reached us in this way, words like *illustrate, transportation,* and *speculate.*

The Romans themselves had borrowed many words from the Greeks. Some of the Greek words had been borrowed from still earlier people, the Phoenicians. Today we use many words from Greek, including *philosophy, photography, physiology, hydrometer,* and many other scientific words. This Greek influence brought the period of Modern English, from 1500 C.E. to the present.

Here is one way of representing the contributions of the Anglo-Saxon, Latin, and Greek languages to English.

Draw the *Layers of the English Language* triangle on the board and fill it in as follows:

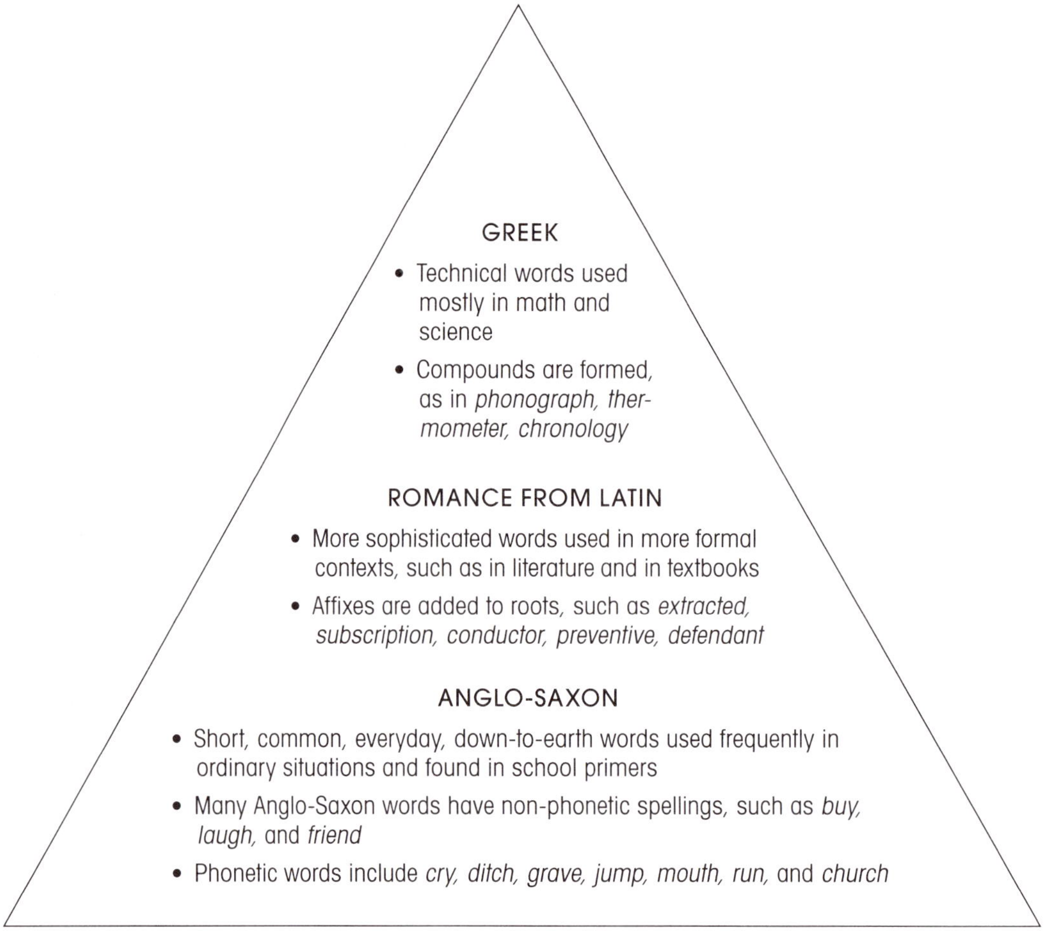

GREEK

- Technical words used mostly in math and science
- Compounds are formed, as in *phonograph, thermometer, chronology*

ROMANCE FROM LATIN

- More sophisticated words used in more formal contexts, such as in literature and in textbooks
- Affixes are added to roots, such as *extracted, subscription, conductor, preventive, defendant*

ANGLO-SAXON

- Short, common, everyday, down-to-earth words used frequently in ordinary situations and found in school primers
- Many Anglo-Saxon words have non-phonetic spellings, such as *buy, laugh,* and *friend*
- Phonetic words include *cry, ditch, grave, jump, mouth, run,* and *church*

Figure 3.1. Layers of the English language. From *The Book: Components of Reading Instruction* (Unpublished manuscript) (p. 24), by R. C. Calfee and Associates, 1981, CA: Stanford University. Copyright 1981 by R. C. Calfee and Associates. Adapted with permission.

People continue to coin new words. Think of words like *airhead, microwave, proactive, subprime*, and *infomercial.* Other new words enter the English language through the Internet (e.g., *blog*). Words that appear there can often become part of the language if they catch on with a large number of people.

Closing

- **Let's review the historical origins of English writing. What were some of the first forms of writing?** (*cave drawings, pictographs, hieroglyphics, logographs, ideograms*)
- **What are the major word origins found in English words?** (*Anglo-Saxon, Latin, Greek*)
- **During the next several lessons, you will learn more about the three language bases and how each differs from the others.**

Follow-Up

- Have students complete the activities in Handout 3.1.

Handout

3.1 Introduction to Layers of Language

Reminders

The majority of English words come from three language origins: Anglo-Saxon, Latin, and Greek.

The major periods of English are Old English, Middle English, and Modern English.

Activities

1. Draw some objects important in your life as if you were drawing on a cave wall or on a rock.

2. Anglo-Saxon words first appeared in which period of the English language?
 Old English

3. The Latin-based words we use today came about in which period of the English language? **Middle English**

4. The Greek-based words we use today came about in which period of the English language? **Modern English**

5. New words continue to form in English each year. What are some of the newest words you have learned?
 ________ ________ ________ ________

6. If you have a home computer or laptop:
   - Go to www.ancientscripts.com. Spend some time inspecting this interesting Web site. You might first want to click on Origins of Writing.
   - Check out http://logos.uoregon.edu/explore/orthography for excellent examples of Chinese logographs.
   - Go to www.KryssTal.com/writing.html. Under Tables and Charts, click on Evolution of the Latin Alphabet. Write your name in Phoenician and Greek, forerunners of the Latin alphabet used today.

Lesson 3.2 Anglo-Saxon Letter-Sound Correspondences and Syllable Patterns

Opening

Today we will study the Anglo-Saxon layer of the English language in order to learn more about the words we use that come from that source. We will review the common Anglo-Saxon letter-sound correspondences and syllable patterns.

Objective

Students will learn about English words stemming from the Anglo-Saxon layer of language.

Procedure

Anglo-Saxon Letter-Sound Correspondences

As you were first learning to read, you started out reading words from the Anglo-Saxon base of the language. These were the everyday, frequently used, short words that are typical in primers and children's stories. The Anglo-Saxon-based words generally have only one or two syllables. In Unit 1, we talked about how we organize the letter-sound correspondences for most of these words: We talked about consonants, vowels, blends, consonant and vowel digraphs, and *r*- and *l*-controlled vowels. Review the Anglo-Saxon letter-sound correspondence chart (see Table O.2) used in Unit 1. See if students have specific questions about any section. You may want to reintroduce less common patterns, such as *wr, kn,* and *dge.*

Write the following words on the board. Let's review some of the patterns found in the following words. See if you can *read* the word and *identify* consonants, vowels, blends, consonant and vowel digraphs, and *r*- and *l*-controlled vowels.

branch	track	blink	crawl
round	spoil	cart	charm
porch	made	seen	play

Anglo-Saxon Syllable Patterns

In Unit 2, we talked about several kinds of syllable patterns. These patterns work well with short two- or three-syllable Anglo-Saxon words. Let's review where we would divide the following words. Write the following words on the board and discuss syllable division with the class.

rabbit	napkin	Halloween	crazy
hamster	velvet	after	spigot
hundred	trumpet	candle	table
grumble	violin	hobo	teamster

Spell **the following multisyllabic words and phrases as I dictate them to you:**

frizzle	starlet	boundary	pilot
grumpy triplets	simple puzzle	twisting acrobat	mushy cucumber

Closing

- **What language layer did we study today?** (*Anglo-Saxon*)
- **What do you know about words from this layer?** (*came from Old English; usually short, common, everyday words*)
- **What patterns did we review?** (*letter-sound correspondences and syllable patterns*)

Follow-Up

- Have students look for common Anglo-Saxon–based words in their literature books.
- Have students complete the activities in Handout 3.2.

UNIT 3
36

Handout 3.2 Anglo-Saxon Letter-Sound Correspondences and Syllable Patterns

Reminder

Common Anglo-Saxon words often contain consonant blends, consonant digraphs, and vowel digraphs (or vowel teams).

Activities

1. Find 10 Anglo-Saxon–based words in literature, in your social studies textbook, or in a magazine. List them and tell why you think they are Anglo-Saxon.

Ex: *friend* (short, irregular) ______________________ Ex: *stop* (common, everyday, short)

______________________ ______________________

______________________ ______________________

______________________ ______________________

______________________ ______________________

______________________ ______________________

2. Draw lines from syllables in the first column to syllables in the second column to make real words:

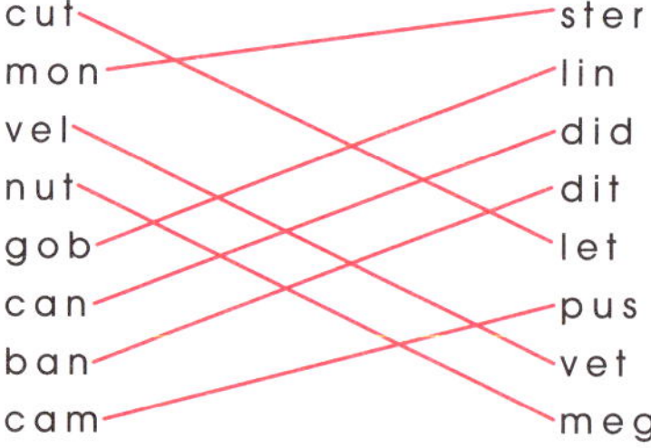

Lesson 3.3 Anglo-Saxon Morpheme Patterns (Compound Words)

Opening

Today we will again study the Anglo-Saxon layer of the English language in order to learn more about the words we use that come from that source. We will learn about a new set of common patterns, the *morpheme* patterns used to expand words. A morpheme is the smallest unit of meaning in English words. Today we will study Anglo-Saxon compound words, and in the next two lessons, we will study adding prefixes and then suffixes to Anglo-Saxon base words.

Objective

Students will learn about expanding words into compound words by combining two base words of Anglo-Saxon origin.

Procedure

Compound Words

Many words in English are compounds of simpler units; both their pronunciation and their meaning are easier to figure out if complex words can be broken into their basic morphemic elements or parts. Anglo-Saxon words are often made up of two smaller base words. When the base words are put together, they form what are called *compound words.* Compounding is one of the major ways by which English words are created. For instance, *waste* combines with *basket* to become *waste-basket,* and *flash* combines with *light* to become *flashlight.* The meaning of the compound word will have something to do with each of the base words. Note that in an Anglo-Saxon compound word, each base word can stand alone.

Write several compound words (see list below) on the board. Ask students how the words are alike (all have two small words and are compounds). Then have students read the compound words and give you the two base words.

outlaw	washcloth	headquarters	blackboard
toothbrush	overpass	railroad	touchdown
silverware	watchman	splashdown	wristwatch
airline	thunderstorm	sunflower	jellyfish
toenail	newsboy	fishhook	peppermint
earthquake	grandfather	backpack	baseball

Have students generate compound words of their own to add to the list.

Dictate the following words and phrases to your students for them to **spell**:

grandchild	stagehand	starfish	sleepwalk
blackbird	floorboard	housecoat	slingshot
playing football	rushing waterfall	messy paperwork	loud thunderstorm
bright sunrise	homesick girls	strawberry pie	southwest cowboy

Closing

- **What did we do today?** (*learned about compound words; combined two Anglo-Saxon base words to make a longer compound word; read and spelled compound words*)

Follow-Up

- Have students complete the activities in Handout 3.3.

Handout 3.3 Anglo-Saxon Morpheme Patterns (Compound Words)

Reminders

Morphemes are the smallest unit of meaning in English words.

Anglo-Saxon-based words can combine two short base words as one means of word expansion. This is called *compounding*.

Activities

1. Match the base words in column 1 with the base words in column 2 to make compound words:

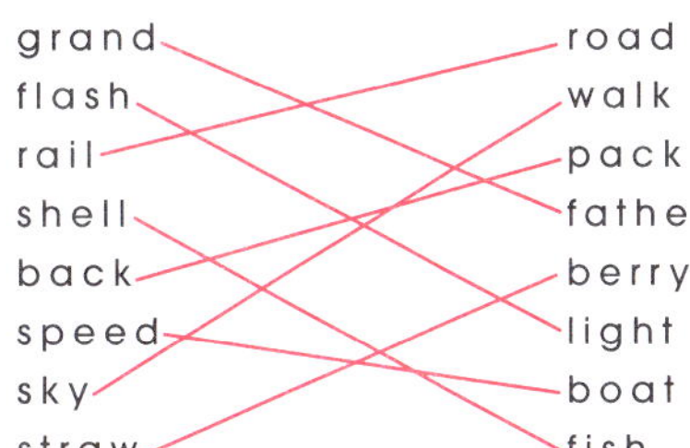

2. Write any 10 compound words below:

Lesson

3.4 Anglo-Saxon Morpheme Patterns (Prefixes)

Opening

Today we will continue our study of Anglo-Saxon morphemes. We will expand words by adding prefixes to Anglo-Saxon base words.

Objective

Students will learn about common prefixes added to Anglo-Saxon base words. They will read and spell numerous words with prefixes.

Procedure

English words are also extended and new words created through the process of adding prefixes and suffixes. This is known as *affixation*. Today we'll work on common prefixes that have meanings of their own. Prefixes cannot stand alone; they come at the beginning of a word (e.g., *rewind*). Point out that the main word to which prefixes and affixes are affixed is called the *base* or *base word*. In this manual, the term *root* has been reserved for Latin word roots.

Prefixes

Write the words below on the board and have students underline the prefix in each word. **Here is a list of words. See if you can find the prefixes in these words. First, underline the prefix, and then read the word.** Point out the prefixes at the beginning of each word if students are unable to find the prefixes.

forearm	exchange	subway	disclose
inside	alone	befriend	adrift
unhappy	defog	unlike	dislike
alike	amount	aground	recall
return	delight	preview	forecast
misplace	prefix	refresh	preplan

Each prefix holds specific meaning. Here are the meanings of some commonly used prefixes. Notice the prefix *a* usually has the schwa sound (the vowel in an unstressed syllable). You can sound out most other prefixes, as you know the syllable types.

a /ə/ = on, in, to	*dis* = not, absence of	*in* = in, not	*mis* = bad, wrong
un = not	*fore* = before	*ex* = out	*non* = not, negative
sub = under, below	*re* = back, again	*be* = completely	*pre* = before
de = down, away			

Spell the following words as I dictate them to you. Underline the prefix in each word.

rethink	subsoil	predate	misspell	nonsense
unhappy	express	discount	befriend	income

Closing

- **What did we do today?** (*studied common Anglo-Saxon prefixes; read and spelled words with prefixes and bases*)

Follow-Up

- **Look for prefixes in words in your textbooks. See how many you can find.**
- Have students complete the activities in Handout 3.4.

Handout 3.4 Anglo-Saxon Morpheme Patterns (Prefixes)

Reminder

A prefix is a morpheme with special meaning that comes at the beginning of a word. By adding a prefix, a new word is created with changed meaning or function.

Activities

1. Add *pre-* or *re-* to make real words:

pre school	re group
re call	re tire
pre flight	pre plan

2. Add *in-* or *un-* to make real words:

un like	un happy
in side	un less
in field	un fair

3. Match the prefix with the correct meaning:

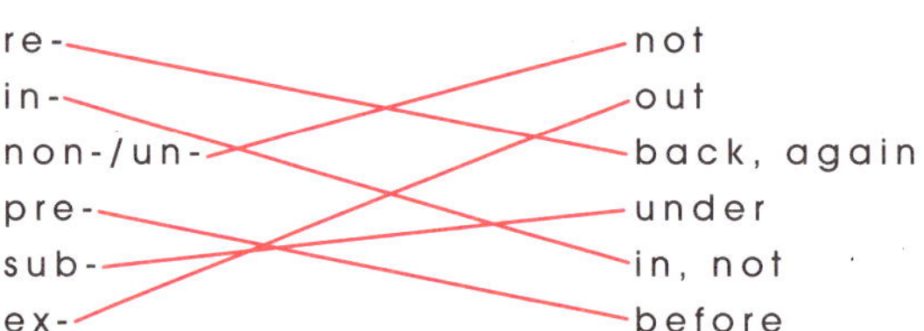

Lesson

3.5 Anglo-Saxon Morpheme Patterns (Suffixes)

Opening

Today we'll talk about the morphemes added to the end of Anglo-Saxon base words. They are called *suffixes*.

Objective

Students will learn about common suffixes added to Anglo-Saxon base words. They will read and spell numerous words with suffixes.

Procedure

Here are some common Anglo-Saxon suffixes. Tell me some words that have these endings, and I'll write them on the board.

-*ed* (past tense verb)	-*er* (noun; adjective)	-*ing* (noun; verb; adjective)	-*ly* (adverb)
-*s* (-*es*) (plural noun; present tense verb)	-*able* (adjective)	-*hood* (noun)	-*ful* (adjective)
-*less* (adjective)	-*ness* (noun)	-*ship* (noun)	-*est* (adjective)

Suffixes add grammatical meaning to a base word. That is, they put a word into a specific part of speech. For example, -*ed* is used as a past tense ending, as in *heated, dreamed,* and *walked* (notice the three different pronunciations for -*ed*). The suffixes -*s* and -*es* are added for plural nouns (e.g., *cats, churches*) and for present tense verbs (*walks, marches*).

NOTE: Add parts of speech to the list above, as indicated in parentheses.

Now, let's make words with both Anglo-Saxon prefixes and suffixes. You tell me some words, and I'll write them on the board. Then we'll read them together, for example, *precooked, unlikely, rereading*.)

NOTE: Point out that compound words can also be affixed (e.g., *lonesome, lonesomeness*).

Spelling Rules for Adding Suffixes

When we add suffixes, we often have to pay attention to three spelling rules.

NOTE: Many teachers prefer to teach these rules in three or four separate sessions.

1. The Silent-*e* Rule

When adding suffixes beginning with a vowel to words ending in a silent *e*, the *e* is dropped. The long vowel sound is retained. Present the following words for students to **spell** as you dictate them.

care	cared	caring	careless
like	liked	likable	likely
safe	safer	safest	safely
time	timed	timing	timely
use	used	using	useful

In order to retain the soft sound of *c* and *g*, keep the silent *e* when adding the suffixes *-able* and *-ous*. Write the following list on the board and discuss with students what would happen if the *e* was dropped.

changeable	traceable	enforceable	chargeable
courageous	outrageous	peaceable	replaceable

Also, the final *e* is kept in some cases to save the identity of the word. Write the following list on the board and discuss with students what would happen if the *e* was dropped.

singeing	hoeing	shoeing	acreage
tingeing	dyeing	canoeing	mileage

2. The Doubling Rule

A. One-syllable base words

When a base word ends with a single consonant preceded by a vowel, double the final consonant if the suffix begins with a vowel. Write the words in column 1 on the board. Add the suffix and ask students if the final consonant in the base word should be doubled (e.g., *sad* + *er* = *sadder*).

sad	sadder	saddest
strap	strapped	strapping
fit	fitter	fittest
drop	dropper	dropping

This doubling rule relates to the vowel markers we discussed in Unit 1. If there was just one consonant, the preceding vowel would be long (e.g., *hopping* vs. *hoping*).

Words ending in two consonants, or having a vowel digraph, do not double a final consonant, because the vowel sound is already established. Write the base words on the board. Then write the suffix and ask students if the final consonant in the base word should be doubled (e.g., *dust* + *y* = *dusty*).

dust	dusty
chant	chanting
last	lasted
cool	cooler
boil	boiling
deep	deepest

Also, you needn't double the final consonant if the suffix begins with a consonant. Write the base words on the board. Then write the suffix and ask students if the final consonant in the base word should be doubled (e.g., *hot* + *ly* = *hotly*).

hot	hotly
ship	shipment
fret	fretful
slim	slimness
drip	dripless
glad	gladly

B. Polysyllabic base words

NOTE: This is probably the most difficult rule for students with learning disabilities to understand. It is recommended that you not include it until the upper grades.

The doubling rule also applies to words of two or more syllables, provided that the accent falls on the last syllable and the conditions discussed earlier are met.

Write the base word on the board. Then write the suffix. Determine where the accent is in the word. Discuss why the final consonant in the base word is or is not doubled.

begin'	beginning	beginner
forbid'	forbidden	forbidding
But: o'pen	opened	opening
transmit'	transmitting	transmitted
excel'	excelled	excelling
But: mar'ket	marketed	marketing

NOTE: If you have students that can't hear accent, don't dwell on this problem. Let students know that most Latin roots get the accent, thus will double the consonant (this will be covered in Unit 4). On the other hand, words with no common root (often of Anglo-Saxon origin) will not have the accent on the last syllable. For example, *mar'ket, marketed; gar'den, gardening; o'pen, opening.*

3. The Final-*y* Rule

A. Words ending in *y* preceded by a vowel just add the suffix.

Write the base word on the board and add the suffix. Discuss why the suffix is added with no change in the base word.

play	played	player
buy	buyer	buying
enjoy	enjoyable	enjoyment
stray	straying	strayed

B. Words ending in *y* preceded by a consonant change the *y* to *i* when adding a suffix, unless the suffix begins with the letter *i*.

Write the base word on the board and add the suffix. Discuss why you should or shouldn't change the *y* to *i*.

empty	emptied	(emptying)
silly	sillier	
easy	easily	
spy	spied	(spying)
copy	copier	(copyist)
early	earliest	
apply	appliance	(applying)
victory	victorious	
fry	fried	(frying)
fly	flier	(flying)

Present the following words and phrases for students to **spell** as you dictate them.

respelled	untimely	preheating	hopefulness
walking slowly	blameless coaches	played harder	greenest lawns
stopping	blaming	grinning	hoping
hottest flames	timing the game	biggest boys	slimy frogs

Closing

- **What did we study today?** (*suffixes and suffix addition rules*)
- **Who can summarize the three rules for adding suffixes?** (*Rule 1: Dropping final* e*—When a base word ends with final* e*, drop the* e *before adding a suffix starting with a vowel; Rule 2: Double-letter rule—(a) one-syllable words: In a one-syllable word, with one short vowel ending in one consonant, double the final consonant before a suffix starting with a vowel (-ed., -er, -ing, -y, etc.) and (b) polysyllabic words: The above rule applies to the final syllable in a polysyllabic word if the final syllable is accented; Rule 3: Base words ending in* y*—When a base word ends with* y*, change the* y *to* i *before adding a suffix unless the* y *is preceded by a vowel or unless the suffix begins with an* i)
- **Name two ways that Anglo-Saxon words expand.** (*by compounding (i.e., putting two base words together) and by affixing (i.e., adding prefixes and suffixes to base words)*)

Follow-Up

- Ask students to look for common prefixes and suffixes in their literature books.
- Have students complete the activities in Handout 3.5.

Handout

3.5 Anglo-Saxon Morpheme Patterns (Suffixes)

Reminders

A suffix is a morpheme added to the end of a word to change the part of speech of a base word.

Some suffixes have specific meanings, while others have vague meanings.

Activities

1. Circle the suffixes in these sentences:

   The tiger(s) jump(ed) into the gold(en) ring.

   He quiet(ly) help(ed) the friend(ly) skat(er).

   She care(less)(ly) misplac(ed) her earring(s).

2. Recalling the rules for suffix addition, spell the following words in the space provided:

care + less = careless	cry + ed = cried
big + est = biggest	blame + less = blameless
blame + ing = blaming	mud + y = muddy
swim + er = swimmer	skate + er = skater
try + ed = tried	baby + ing = babying
baby + ed = babied	green + est = greenest
hope + less = hopeless	hope + ing = hoping
slime + y = slimy	slim + er = slimmer

Lesson 3.6 Anglo-Saxon Non-Phonetic Words

Opening

Today we continue our study of the Anglo-Saxon layer of the English language. We will learn about words that do not follow the common letter-sound correspondences. We call these *non-phonetic words.*

Objective

Students will learn about Anglo-Saxon non-phonetic words, those words that must be memorized for reading and spelling them.

Procedure

It is somewhat unfortunate that many of the Anglo-Saxon words you learn first are often weirdly spelled words like *though, through, rough, ought,* and *bough.* These words all have *o-u-g-h* in them, but the sound of *o-u-g-h* is different in each word. These common words that do not follow regular letter-sound correspondence are often called *irregular words, non-phonetic words, rote memory words,* or, more simply, *weirdo words.*

Here are a few of the more than 100 irregular English words. Can you read them? Write the following words on the board.

was	want	love	often
one	once	only	build
said	who	whom	friend
what	were	where	tough
laugh	through	would	could
cough	pretty	floor	eye
does	from	they	says

NOTE: Ask students why the words are irregular. Point out that the vowel sound is usually the difficult part, as it isn't what the reader expects. Consonants generally retain their regular sound. (See the Non-Phonetic Words list in this manual.) These words should be memorized for both reading and spelling. Assign five or so words each week.

NOTE: Students who have trouble memorizing the irregular, non-phonetic words should be encouraged to trace and copy the words, saying each letter name and then the whole word. These words must be rote memorized, as students cannot count on one-to-one letter-sound association, especially for the vowels.

Have students spell several irregular words in phrases or short sentences:

through the forest	*Who* was the boy?
only one tree	*laugh* or cry
They were in *love.*	*I want* a cat.

Closing

- **What kind of Anglo-Saxon words did we study today?** (*non-phonetic words*)
- **How do they differ from most of the other short Anglo-Saxon words we have studied?** (*they have to be memorized; the vowel sound isn't regular*)

Follow-Up

- To show students how frequently the irregular words are used in text, have the children find as many of these words as possible in one page of text. This activity works well with small groups.
- Have students complete the activities in Handout 3.6.

Handout 3.6 Anglo-Saxon Non-Phonetic Words

Reminders

Many of the English words from the Anglo-Saxon layer of language are non-phonetic words. That is, they cannot be sounded out by using regular letter-sound correspondence.

Usually the vowel sound in non-phonetic words is irregular.

Activities

1. Here is a group of Anglo-Saxon words. Some are phonetically regular words and some are non-phonetic. Circle the non-phonetic words:

were	blue	sky	**said**
laugh	flat	smart	scrape
tough	**done**	bone	**only**
sled	**two**	crock	**want**
where	**whose**	chose	**sugar**
you	**pretty**	stretch	**have**

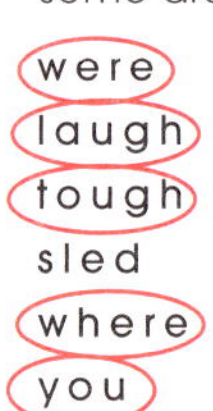

2. Write 3 sentences using at least 2 of the following non-phonetic words in each sentence:

friend	through	cough	build	once
what	who	often	love	hour

- ____
- ____
- ____

Lesson

3.7 Summary of the Anglo-Saxon Influence on English

Opening

Today we'll summarize the Anglo-Saxon influence on English writing. Remember that the Anglo-Saxon-based words are usually short, common, everyday, down-to-earth words.

Objective

Students will review the six categories for Anglo-Saxon letter-sound correspondences, the various syllable patterns, and common morpheme patterns.

Procedure

Do you remember the chart with the major categories of Anglo-Saxon letter-sound correspondences? Show a blank 3 x 2 matrix with category headings (see Table 1.1). You'll recall that letters are either consonants or vowels. Consonants can be single letters or combinations of consonants, as in consonant blends and consonant digraphs. Give me some suggestions of single consonants, consonant blends, and consonant digraphs to fill in the blank cells. Write these in Table 1.1.

Vowels can also be placed in one of three cells: single-letter short and long vowels, *r*-controlled vowels, and vowel digraphs. Tell me the vowel letters and their short sounds. What are the long vowel sounds? Let's fill in the blanks with *r*-controlled vowels and vowel digraphs.

Remember, also, that the Anglo-Saxon layer contains many irregular short words, for example, *one, was, would, their, cough,* and *friend.* Can you think of other nonphonetic (or weirdo) words?

Review with students the six syllable types and common patterns for syllable division. Also see if students recall the common prefixes and suffixes covered earlier in this unit. Let them know that in the next lessons, they will be learning about the Latin and Greek layers of the English language.

NOTE: Lessons on dictionary use are not included but should be addressed. Be sure students know how to use the alphabetical keywords and understand diacritical markings. Have dictionaries that contain etymological information in your classroom.

Closing

- What are the characteristics of words of Anglo-Saxon origin? (short, everyday, down-to-earth words; the first words we learn in school; found in school primers; often have irregular spellings)
- Name several common non-phonetic words (e.g., *none, does, laugh, friend, want, what*)

Follow-Up

- Have students complete the activities in Handout 3.7.

Handout 3.7 Summary of the Anglo-Saxon Influence on English

Reminder

The Anglo-Saxon-based words in English are those short, common, everyday words we use frequently in both speech and text. These short words expand by both compounding and affixing (adding prefixes and/or suffixes).

Activities

1. Write 3 sentences using only one-syllable words:
   - ______________________________
   - ______________________________
   - ______________________________

2. Write 8 compound words:

______________	______________
______________	______________
______________	______________
______________	______________

3. Divide the following words into syllables:

puz|zle	in|dex	fo|cus	ath|lete
car|bon	ze|ro	un|der|mine	spin|dle
stam|pede	tur|pen|tine	fan|tas|tic	ta|ble
bub|ble	in|ter|lude	se|quel	yes|ter|day

Lesson

3.8 Latin Letter-Sound Correspondences

Opening

Today we begin our study of the Latin layer of the English language. Most of the words in this layer come to us from the Latin language spoken in ancient Rome, and in Latium, an ancient country in Italy. These words, too, have letter-sound correspondences, syllable patterns, and morpheme patterns. Some patterns are similar to those of Anglo-Saxon, but some patterns are different.

Objective

Students will learn about words of Latin origin and about the Latin-based letter-sound correspondences. They will read words of Latin origin and learn about the schwa found in many Latin-based words.

Procedure

We'll be reading words of Latin origin and looking for common patterns. In future lessons, you'll learn much more about Latin syllable and morpheme patterns.

Usually students encounter Latin-based words in third grade, after having considerable experience with Anglo-Saxon words. Your knowledge of consonants and vowels transfers directly to words of Latin origin. Fortunately, you will find few of the complex Anglo-Saxon digraphs.

Latin is the basis for all Romance languages. These languages include French, Italian, Portuguese, Romanian, and Spanish. The majority of English words come from this layer of language. It is estimated that about 55% of English words are Latin-based.

Latin-based words are usually multisyllabic, as they contain a root and a prefix and/or suffix. The root generally gets the stress, or accent. The most notable feature about Latin words is the vowel sound pronounced as a schwa—somewhat like the sound of the *a* in *about.* The schwa is a neutral vowel sound found in unaccented syllables. The sign for a schwa (the diacritical dictionary marking) is /ə/. You'll find the schwa in prefixes and suffixes and other unaccented syllables that are not as important as the root words (e.g., *servant, attractive, dentist*).

Write the following words on the board. Let's *read* the following words and underline the schwa sounds in each word:

machine	immigrant	attendant	excellent
predicate	committee	selection	turbulent
allowance	instrument	intractable	incredible

NOTE: Words with the schwa sound may not be difficult to read, as students usually read in context. However, the schwa may cause problems in spelling, as the speller does not hear a true vowel sound.

Closing

- **What is the schwa sound?** (*the neutral vowel in an unaccented syllable*)
- **What are the differences in the Latin and Anglo-Saxon letter-sound correspondences?** (*vowel and consonant sounds are the same in words of both origins; Latin-based words contain relatively few vowel digraphs; many Latin-based words have the schwa sound, as they are usually multisyllabic words*)
- **Why should we study the words of Latin origin?** (*these words make up over 50% of words in English; they are often found in literature and content-area textbooks*)

Follow-Up

- Have students complete the activities in Handout 3.8.

Handout

3.8 Latin Letter-Sound Correspondences

Reminders

No new letter-sound correspondences are introduced in the Latin layer of language, but the schwa appears often. The schwa is the neutral vowel sound in an unaccented syllable.

Because Latin roots are affixed, the affixes are usually schwaed because they are not accented.

Activities

1. Circle the schwa sounds in the following words:

attractive	excellent	deportment	observant
conformist	governess	vigorous	direction

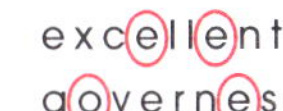

2. List words from a newspaper, magazine, or textbook that contain the schwa sound.

Ex: aggressive ______ ______ ______

______ ______ ______ ______

______ ______ ______ ______

Lesson

3.9 Latin Syllable Patterns

Opening

Today we'll study the common Latin syllable patterns and divide words into syllables.

Objective

Students will study the common Latin syllable patterns and how Latin-based words are divided into syllables.

Procedure

Syllable patterns are generally the same in Latin-based words as they are in words of Anglo-Saxon origin. The VCCV, VCV, and VCCCV patterns are common. Prefixes and suffixes often consist of closed or open syllables. Here are some Romance words with typical syllable patterns. Let's read them and divide the words into syllables. Write the following words on the board.

interrupt	traction	enterprise	introduce	rival
prediction	identity	nonreflective	literature	instrumentalist
reception	eruption	captivity	respectful	circumscribe

Closing

- **Remember that words of Latin origin will be divided similarly to those of Anglo-Saxon origin.**

Follow-Up

- Have students complete the activities in Handout 3.9.

Handout 3.9 Latin Syllable Patterns

Reminder

Syllable patterns remain the same regardless of a word's origin. The VCCV, VCCCV, and VCV patterns are often found in words of Latin origin.

Activities

1. Count the number of syllables in the following words and write it on the line:

introduce 3	population 4	reconstruct 3
spectator 3	circumnavigate 5	accomplishment 4
collective 3	predominate 4	superstition 4
retrospective 4	obstructionist 4	illegible 4

2. Divide the following words into syllables:

col|lec|tion	in|ter|rupt	de|struc|tive	dis|rup|ted
tact|ful|ness	in|ten|ded	un|der|stand|a|ble	ver|dict
pre|dic|tion	cir|cum|flex	re|flec|ting	trans|fix

Lesson

3.10 Latin Morpheme Patterns

Opening

Remember that morphemes are the wordlike meaning units in a word. Latin-based words have numerous prefixes, root words, and suffixes that make up thousands of words. These word parts are valuable not only for decoding and spelling but also for increasing our vocabulary knowledge.

Objective

Students will learn about common Latin morphemes. They will read and spell words containing Latin morphemes.

Procedure

In this lesson, you will be introduced to many of the Latin morphemes. In Unit 4, you will have opportunities to discuss the specific meaning of these morphemes and to read and spell numerous words.

Latin Roots

The root word is usually stressed, as it contains the major meaning of the word. Let's read the following common root words. You should be able to sound them out easily, as they follow regular letter-sound correspondence. Write the following root words on the board.

spect	flect	lit	rupt	scribe (script)
duct	vis	gress	struct	aud
dict	pend	vent	tract	ped

Ask students to generate a few words using the roots listed above.

Latin Prefixes

Write the following Latin prefixes on the board. **The Latin-based prefixes are also usually regular. Here are some common Latin prefixes for you to *read*.** See if students can generate words using these prefixes.

re	sub	pre	il	dis
extra	bi	inter	per	pro
intro	ultra	mid	infra	trans

Latin Suffixes

Suffixes usually place a word into a specific part of speech. For example, words ending in *-or* = noun; *-ist* = noun (person); *-ar, -ous, -ive* = adjective; and *-ify* = verb.

Suffixes often have the schwa sound, as they are unstressed. Here are some words with suffixes. Can you find the schwas? Underline the schwas as I write each word on the board.

excellent	servant	generous
necessity	important	moment
service	possible	manage

A special instance of this pattern shows up in words like:

nation	omission	musician
precious	partial	prediction
pretentious	vacation	spatial

The vowel digraphs in the suffixes above are all pronounced as schwas. In addition, notice that all the initial consonants in the suffixes—all followed by *i*—are pronounced like /sh/ in *shut.*

Closing

- **What did we study today?** (Latin morphemes: prefixes, roots, and suffixes)
- **Remember that many of the longer words you use in the upper grades are of Latin origin.** Review the similarities and differences in Latin- and Anglo-Saxon-based words. (*same letter-sound correspondences in words of both origins, but common presence of the schwa in unaccented prefixes and suffixes in Latin-based words*)

Follow-Up

- Have students look for multisyllabic Latin-based words in their social studies textbooks.
- Have students complete the activities in Handout 3.10.

Handout

3.10 Latin Morpheme Patterns

Reminders

Latin root words always affix to make longer words. We add prefixes and suffixes to the Latin roots.

The prefixes and suffixes are often schwaed in Latin words, as they are usually in unstressed syllables.

Activities

1. Circle the prefixes in the following Latin-based words:

conducive	reflection	circumference	transmitted
ambidextrous	interaction	pretention	accumulate
submarine	obstructed	retrospective	suffix

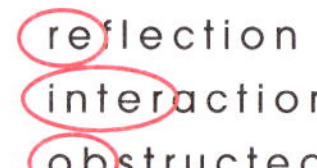

2. Circle the roots in the following Latin-based words:

predicted	conductor	invented	audition
instruction	informant	important	reflexive
congregate	transmission	collection	expeditious

3. Circle the suffixes in the following Latin-based words:

aggravate	selection *or tion*	magician *or cian*	suspenseful
inventor	dentist	patronage	permissive
incredible	contingent	gradual	standardize

Lesson

3.11 Greek Letter-Sound Correspondences

Opening

Today we will study the Greek layer of the English language. Words of Greek origin are usually specialized words used in math and science, though some are common, for example, *television*. Like words from the Anglo-Saxon and Latin layers, Greek words have letter-sound correspondences, syllable patterns, and morpheme patterns. We will look at some of the similarities and differences as we read many words from the Greek layer of language.

Objective

Students will learn about the Greek layer of language, especially the unique letter-sound correspondences.

Procedure

Words of Greek origin use the same letter-sound correspondences as those in Anglo-Saxon words, but add three important new patterns: *ch* pronounced as /k/, *ph* pronounced as /f/, and the use of *y* as a long vowel /ī/ or short vowel /ĭ/.

Write the following words on the board and have students look for the element that is noticeably Greek.

photograph	sympathy	phonograph	synthesis	hydrogen
architect	physiology	philosophy	hydrophone	chronology
chloroplast	monocycle	chronology	chromoscope	astrophysics

Greek words often contain a silent *p* in the *pn, ps,* and *pt* pattern (as in *pneumonia, pseudonym,* and *pterodactyl*). In addition, *mn* (as in *mnemonics*) and *rh* (as in *rhinoplasty*) are Greek forms.

Closing

- What did we study today? (*Greek letter-sound correspondences*)
- Who can tell me some of the unique Greek letter-sound correspondences? (ch, ph, y *as short or long vowel,* pn, ps, pt, mn, rh)
- In what subject areas will you find numerous Greek-based words? (*math and science*)

Follow-Up

- Have students look for Greek-based words in their math and science books. See if they can use the unique letter-sound correspondences as clues.
- Have students complete the activities in Handout 3.11.

Handout 3.11 Greek Letter-Sound Correspondences

Reminders

The Greek layer of language contains some unique letter-sound correspondences. The most common are *ph* for the /f/ sound, *ch* for the /k/ sound, and *y* for the /ĭ/ or /ī/ sound.

Less common combinations are *pn* (/n/), *mn* (/n/), *rh* /r/, and *ps* /s/.

Activities

1. Circle the unique Greek letter-sound correspondences in the following words. Try to read the words:

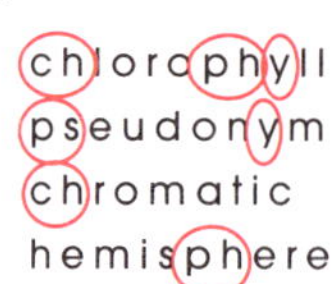

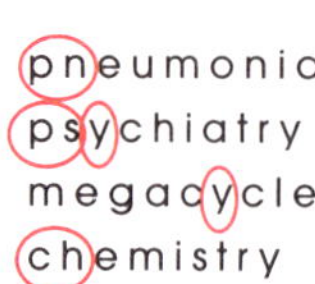

2. Look for Greek letter-sound correspondences in words you find in your science textbook. Try to read the words. List them here

Ex: hydrosphere ____ ____ ____

____ ____ ____ ____

____ ____ ____ ____

Lesson

3.12 Greek Syllable Patterns

Opening

Today we'll study the Greek syllable patterns. We'll practice dividing Greek-based words into syllables.

Objective

Students will learn about common Greek syllable patterns and divide words into syllables.

Procedure

Words of Greek origin can be divided into syllables just like words of Anglo-Saxon or Latin origin. Common patterns are VCCV and VCV as in *octa, phono,* and *physio.*

You will also find the CVVC pattern where words are divided between the vowels.

Write the following words on the board. **As you divide the following words into syllables, think about whether the vowel sounds are long or short. Read the words aloud.**

phonograph	orthodontist	system	autograph	hydroplane
periscope	dermatology	hypodermic	physical	symphony
sophomore	cyclone	theology	bioscientist	byrophobia

Closing

- **What did we study today?** (*Greek syllable patterns*)
- **Why is it helpful to be aware of letter-sound correspondences and syllable patterns in Greek-based words?** (*helps to read and spell the words*)

Follow-Up

- Have students complete the activities in Handout 3.12.

Handout 3.12 Greek Syllable Patterns

Reminder

Syllable division in Greek-based words is similar to the Anglo-Saxon- and Latin-based words. In addition, you will often find words with the CVVC pattern in which you divide between the two vowels, as in *sci/en/tist* and *the/ol/o/gy.*

Activities

1. Divide the following Greek-based words into syllables and read the words:

Ne/o/lith/ic	zo/o/l/o/gy	an/to/nym	or/tho/scop/ic
syn/chro/nize	mi/cro/scope	de/moc/ra/cy	bi/cy/cle
chron/o/met/ric	an/thro/pol/o/gy	psy/chi/a/try	di/no/saur

2. List 9 Greek-based words from your science textbook and divide them into syllables. Try to read the words.

______	______	______
______	______	______
______	______	______

Lesson

3.13 Greek Morpheme Patterns

Opening

Words of Greek origin are generally compounded using two main Greek word roots. Today's introduction to Greek morpheme patterns will serve as a basis for the next unit's in-depth discussion of Greek-based words.

Objective

Students will learn about Greek morpheme patterns.

Procedure

Greek words are often made up of two parts with equal stress. Some people call the word parts *roots,* and still others call them *combining forms.* Because the morphemes compound, we'll call them *combining forms.* Write the following words on the board.

Notice that these Greek words have two parts, each of equal importance:

telescope	tele + scope
polygon	poly + gon
psychology	psych + ology
telegram	tele + gram
hemisphere	hemi + sphere
autograph	auto + graph
biography	bio + graph + y
zoology	zo + ology

As you learn more about Greek-based words in Unit 4, you'll find that some of the combining forms are usually used at the beginning and can be considered prefixes (e.g., *auto-*, *tele-*). We can also add suffixes to the Greek-based words (e.g., *hemisphere, hemispheric*). In addition, in Unit 4, we'll study the meaning of each combining form.

Closing

- As we finish this section on the Greek layer of language, let's review some of the key points to remember. *(unique letter-sound correspondences, types of syllables, and combining forms)*

Follow-Up

- Have students read a passage in their science textbook and look for Greek-based words.
- Have students write sentences using Greek-based words.
- Have students complete the activities in Handout 3.13.

Handout 3.13 Greek Morpheme Patterns

Reminder

Two Greek roots usually combine to form words. These roots are often called *combining forms*. Some of these forms act like prefixes (e.g., *tele, auto, hemi*) and some act like suffixes (e.g., *ology, phobia, mania*).

Activities

1. Circle the 2 Greek combining forms in the words below. Try to read the words.

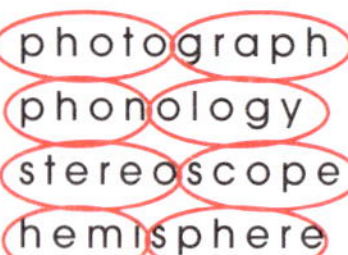

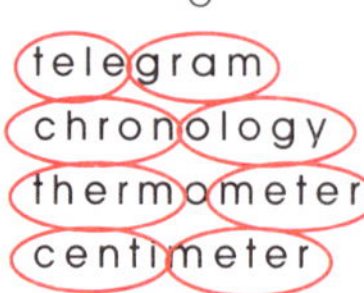

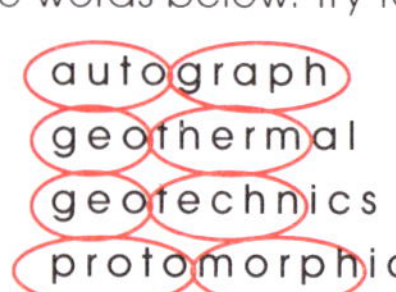

2. Find 12 words in your science and/or math textbook that you think are from the Greek layer of language. List them below:

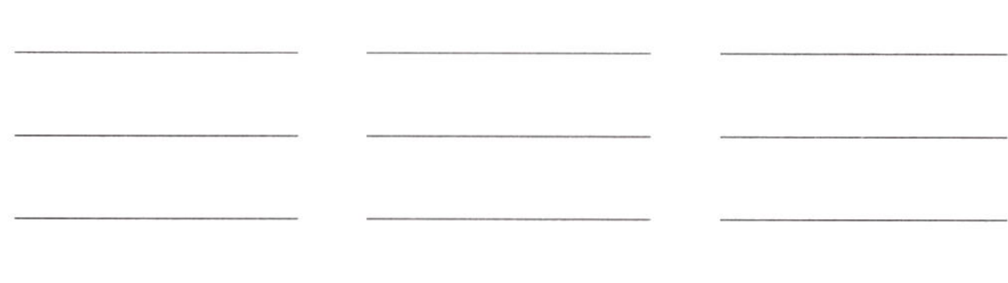

Lesson 3.14 Review of Layers of Language

Opening

Today we'll review the three major language origins for English words and talk about the three key patterns to look at in words.

Objective

Students will review the three most common layers of the English language: Anglo-Saxon, Latin, and Greek.

Procedure

Here is a chart without any headings. I want you to fill it in for me. Who remembers the three layers of language? Write *Anglo-Saxon, Latin,* and *Greek* as headings on the far left side of the blank chart (see Table 3.1).

Who remembers the patterns we need to think about in reading long and/or unfamiliar words? Write *Letter-Sound Correspondences, Syllable Patterns,* and *Morpheme Patterns* across the top of the matrix.

Fill in the chart as students recall the important elements for each cell.

Table 3.1
Word Origin by Word Structure Matrix

WORD ORIGIN	LETTER-SOUND CORRESPONDENCES	SYLLABLE PATTERNS	MORPHEME PATTERNS
ANGLO-SAXON			
ROMANCE based on LATIN			
GREEK			

Closing

- Review with students the purpose for learning about word origins and the three key patterns.

Follow-Up

- Have students complete the activities in Handout 3.14.
- Administer the Unit 3 Quiz found on the CD.

Handout 3.14 Review of Layers of Language

Reminders

In this unit, you learned about the three language origins that most of the English words we use today are from: Anglo-Saxon, Latin, and Greek. Be sure to review the lessons and handouts so you know the different characteristics for the three language origins. As a review for the Unit Quiz, complete the following activities.

Activities

1. Make 5 Anglo-Saxon compound words out of the following base words:

black	hook	grand	foot	board
ball	fish	light	mother	house

fishhook grandmother football blackboard lighthouse

2. Circle the prefixes in the following words:

(re)try	(un)like	(pre)tell	(non)sense
(ex)tract	(sub)way	(dis)place	(in)side

3. Add suffixes to the following base words. (You may want to review Lesson 3.5 for the three suffix-addition rules.)

hope + ing = hoping	hope + less = hopeless
run + ing = running	cry + ing = crying
red + est = reddest	play + ed = played
taste + ful = tasteful	taste + ed = tasted
mud + y = muddy	try + ed = tried

4. Write 5 non-phonetic words in the spaces below.

________ ________ ________ ________ ________

Are non-phonetic words usually irregular in the vowel sound or in the consonant sound? In the vowel sound.

5. Circle the Latin root in each of the following words:

trans(form)ed	in(struct)ed	con(duct)ing
re(flect)ive	im(port)er	pre(vent)ed

6. Circle the 2 Greek combining forms in each of the following words:

(photo)(graph)	(psycho)(logy)	(hemi)(sphere)
(tele)(gram)	(micro)(scope)	(kilo)(meter)

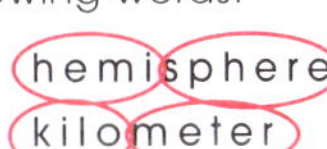

Unit

4 Morpheme Patterns

Lessons

4.1 Latin Prefixes (Open and Closed Syllables)

4.2 Latin Prefixes (Longer Words)

4.3 Latin Chameleon Prefixes

4.4 Latin Suffixes

4.5 Latin Suffixes (/shən/) and More

4.6 Latin Roots (*rupt, port, form, tract, scrib/scribe/script, spec/spect*)

4.7 Latin Roots (*stru/struct, dic/dict, flect/flex, mit/miss*)

4.8 Latin Roots (*cred, duc/duce/duct, pel/puls, pend/pens, fac/fact/fect, vert/vers, ject*)

4.9 Latin Roots (*fer, ven/vent, vid/vis, aud*)

4.10 Greek Combining Forms (34 Common Forms)

4.11 Greek Combining Forms (*phon/phono, photo, graph/gram, auto, tele, log/ology*)

4.12 Greek Combining Forms (*micro, meter, therm, bio, scope, hydro*)

4.13 Greek Combining Forms (*biblio, crat/cracy, geo, metro, pol/polis, dem*)

4.14 Review of Morpheme Patterns

Latin Prefixes (Open and Closed Syllables)

In this unit, we will study morpheme patterns more thoroughly. Morphemes are parts of words that carry meaning. Remember that compound words, prefixes, suffixes, and roots are all morphemes. The Anglo-Saxon and Greek compound words we studied in Unit 3 were made up of two or more morphemes. We will concentrate on important Latin and Greek morphemes in this unit.

Opening

Today we're going to talk about prefixes. Who remembers what a prefix is? (a meaning unit, or morpheme, that comes at the beginning of a word) **You will remember some of these prefixes from Unit 3 (those primarily used with Anglo-Saxon base words). We will read and spell a number of words that contain Latin prefixes.**

Objective

Students will learn common Latin prefixes and their meanings. They will read and spell words containing common Latin prefixes.

Procedure

Here is a list of common prefixes from Latin, along with their meaning. Write the following prefixes on the board.

de- (reverse, remove)	*re-* (back, again)	*pre-* (before)
co- (together, with)	*bi-* (two)	*tri-* (three)
pro- (before, forward)		

Will these prefixes usually have long or short vowel sounds? Why? (*long, because the vowel is at the end of the syllable, making it an open syllable*)

Many prefixes get the schwa sound, /ə/, if they are in unaccented syllables (e.g., *refer, prevent*).

NOTE: Although you will not be focusing on the meaning of prefixes in this lesson, you may want to point out that each prefix has a specific meaning. Students may be able to generate the meaning of many prefixes.

Who can tell me some words that begin with these prefixes? List words under each column on the board as students generate items. Add items of your own to the list. Circle the prefixes.

re-	***pre-***	***pro-***
return	pretend	profound
react	preview	produce
remember	prevent	project
relax		

de-	***bi-***	***co-***
deform	bicycle	coordinate
delight	bilateral	coexist
		cooperate

tri-

triangle

Here is another list of prefixes. Write the following list on the board. **What kind of vowel sound will these words have?** (*short*) **Why?** (*because they are in closed syllables*)

dis- (separation, undoing)	*sub-* (under)	*mis-* (wrong, bad)
in- (in, not)	*im-* (in, not)	*ex-* (out)
trans- (across)	*con-* (together, with)	*non-* (not)

Tell me some words with these prefixes. Write the words students generate on the board and circle the prefixes. Below are some sample words students may generate.

dis-

dislike displace display

in-

invite inline intend

trans-

translate transport transpose

sub-

submarine subway subtract

im-

import improve impact

con-

convict contend convene

mis-

misspell	misplace	misfit

ex-

export	extend	expect

non-

nondescript	nonsense	nonfat

Closing

- **What kind of patterns did we study today?** (*prefixes*)
- **Where do prefixes come in a word?** (*at the beginning of words*)
- **From what language did the prefixes come?** (*Latin*)
- **Why would we want to break a word into its parts?** (*to read and spell words more easily*)
- **How does a prefix change a word?** (*it changes the meaning*)

Follow-Up

- Look for common prefixes in a reading passage. Make a list of these prefixes and generate words using each prefix. Use the dictionary if you wish.
- Have students complete the activities in Handout 4.1.

Handout

4.1 Latin Prefixes (Open and Closed Syllables)

Reminder

Prefixes are meaningful word parts that come at the beginning of a word. Many common prefixes are open or closed syllables.

Activities

1. Match the prefix with its meaning by writing the letter in the space provided:

b.	re	a. three
c.	de	b. back, again
e.	pre	c. reverse, remove
d.	bi	d. two
a.	tri	e. before, forward
f.	co	f. together, with
e.	pro	g. before

2. Add one of the prefixes above to form a word matching the definition:

 co exist (to live in peace with another)
 re develop (to develop again)
 de rail (to run off the rails)
 bi cycle (a two-wheeled vehicle)
 pro vide (to supply or give)
 tri pod (having three legs)
 pre dict (to foretell something)

3. Read each sentence that follows the word list. Write one of the words below to complete each sentence.

retry	replace	reread
retold	replaced	retried
provide	proceed	protect
prepare	prevent	prefer
defy	detour	decode

a. Try to replace the broken chair.

b. The student retold the story to his friend.

c. Please provide your license to the judge.

d. The teacher must ___prepare___ each lesson carefully.

e. Claude can't ___decode___ the difficult words.

4. Match the prefix with its meaning by writing the corresponding letter in the space provided.

e.	dis	a. in, not
g.	sub	b. not
c.	mis	c. bad, wrong
a.	in	d. across
h.	ex	e. not, undo
d.	trans	f. together, with
f.	con	g. under
b.	non	h. out

5. Add one of the prefixes in number 4 to form a word matching the definition:

___dis___arrange (to upset the order of)
___mis___spell (to spell a word incorrectly)
___ex___cuse (to apologize for)
___trans___mit (sending from one person to another)
___non___sense (making no sense)
___sub___normal (less than normal)
___in___flexible (not flexible)
___con___vene (to come together)

6. Read each sentence that follows the word list. Write one of the words below to complete each sentence.

dispute	disturb	disorder
misfire	mistake	misbehave
extract	export	express
transport	translate	transfix
confronted	convention	confident

a. Try not to ___disturb___ the service.

b. The gun can't ___misfire___ with the safety catch on.

c. The dentist will have to ___extract___ my tooth.

d. Please ___translate___ the speech into Spanish for me.

e. The outstanding athlete was ___confident___ he would win.

7. Circle the prefixes in the following words:

return	misspell	preview	displace
protect	recalled	deport	biceps
delight	coordinate	nonsense	translate
expect	submarine	invite	tricycle

8. Add one of the prefixes from the list above to each word part below to complete the story.

The __sub__marine __pro__tected the large harbor. The harbormaster __ex__pected the ships to __re__turn shortly. He __pre__dicted that the sailors would be __de__lighted to be __trans__ported back to their homes in Spain.

Latin Prefixes (Longer Words)

Opening

Today we'll continue learning new Latin prefixes. These will be used in longer words and will often be found in your literature and social studies textbooks.

Objective

Students will learn new Latin prefixes and read and spell words containing them.

Procedure

Here are a few other Latin prefixes. (These are appropriate for the upper grades.)

uni- (one)	*inter-* (among, between)	*intra-* (within, inside)
intro- (into, inward)	*mal-* (bad, evil)	*bene-* (well, good)
post- (after, behind)	*contra-* (against)	*circum-* (around)

Let's read these prefixes and think of some words to write on the board. (Below are some possibilities.)

uni-	***inter-***	***intra-***
uniform	interrupt	intrastate
unicorn	intervene	
unilateral	interact	
	interstate	

intro-	***mal-***	***bene-***
introvert	malnutrition	benefit
introduce	malcontent	benefactor

post-	***contra-***	***circum-***
postdate	contradict	circumference
posthaste	contraband	

Present individual words or dictate several of the following sentences for students to **spell**:

- The boy reported to his teacher.
- He was the best band conductor.
- We attended the meeting.

- The professor informed my teacher.
- We misplaced the bicycle.
- Mother interrupted our conversation.
- I like to add and subtract.
- We exported the cattle.
- We discussed the fantastic story.

Closing

- **What kind of patterns did we study today?** (*prefixes*)
- **From what language did the prefixes come?** (*Latin*)

Follow-Up

- Look for common prefixes in a reading passage. Make a list of these prefixes and generate other words for each prefix. Use the dictionary if you wish.
- Have students complete the activities in Handout 4.2.

Handout 4.2 Latin Prefixes (Longer Words)

Reminder

Some prefixes are used primarily with Latin word roots. They can be one- or two-syllable word parts.

Activities

1. Match the prefix with its meaning by writing the corresponding letter in the space provided:

f. uni	a. within, inside
d. inter	b. well, good
a. intra	c. bad, evil
g. intro	d. among, between
c. mal	e. after, behind
b. bene	f. one
e. post	g. into, inward
i. contra	h. around
h. circum	i. against

2. Complete these sentences using words beginning with a prefix from the list above:
   a. Try not to interrupt your mother while she's talking on the phone.
   b. Wear your Boy Scout uniform to the meeting.
   c. Remember the formula for the circumference of a circle.
   d. The mythical beast, a unicorn, has only one horn.
   e. The starving children suffered from malnutrition.
   f. Highways US 35 and US 80 are interstate highways.
   g. The minister gave the benediction to begin the service.
   h. Please introduce me to your teacher.

3. Add a prefix from number 1 to form a word matching the definition:

mal **content** (a discontented person)
intra **vascular** (within the blood vessels)
inter **personal** (actions between persons)
post **glacial** (after the glacial period)
circum **ference** (the distance around a circle)
contra **dict** (to express the opposite)
uni **lateral** (affecting one side)
intro **vert** (turning inward)
bene **ficial** (enhancing well-being)

Latin Chameleon Prefixes

Opening

We call some prefixes *chameleon* because, just like the lizard, they change depending on what they are next to. That is, they change their spelling depending on the root word to which they are attached.

Objective

Students will learn the variant forms of the chameleon (or, assimilated) prefixes. They will read and spell words containing these prefixes.

Procedure

NOTE: Upper grade teachers should present this information; third-grade teachers should teach this only if they think their students can handle the information.

Note that double consonants often occur with chameleon prefixes (e.g., when prefixes ending in an *l* come before a root beginning with *l*; *r* before *r*; *m* before *m, b,* or *p*, etc.) Here is a list of chameleon prefixes with examples. Write the words on the board as you discuss each. Have students **read** the words.

con- (col-, com-, cor-)

These prefixes mean "together" or "with." Change the *n* to *l* when the root begins with *l*; change the *n* to *r* when the root begins with *r;* and change the *n* to *m* when the root begins with *m, b,* or *p.*

NOTE: These prefixes are rarely accented, so they contain the schwa sound.

con-	***col-***	***com-***
convict	collide	commit
convince	collision	commute
connect	collusion	combine
	collect	compartment
		compound

cor-

correct
corrode
corrosion

in- (il-, im-, ir-)

These prefixes mean "in" or "not." Change the *n* to *l* when the root begins with *l*; change the *n* to *r* when the root begins with *r*; and change the *n* to *m* when the root begins with *m, b,* or *p.*

in-

invite
invent
increase
intend

il-

illegal
illegitimate
illustrate

im-

import
immortal
imbibe
imbalance
impound
important

ir-

irregular
irritate
irresponsible
irresponsive
irrigate
irrigation

sub- (suc-, suf-, sug-, sup-)

These prefixes mean "under." Change the b to c before a root beginning with *c,* to *f* before *f,* to *g* before *g,* and to *p* before *p.*

sub-

subtract
submarine
subway
subject
subjective

suc-

succeed
success
successful

suf-

suffer
suffix
suffuse

sug-

suggest
suggestive

sup-

support
supplant

ad- (ac-, af-, ag-, al-, ap-, ar-, as-, at-)

These prefixes mean "to" or "toward." Change *d* to *f, g, l, p, r, s,* and *t* as follows:

NOTE: The schwa sound appears in many of these words.

ad-

address
addict
admit

ac-

account
accord
accept
accident

af-

afford
affix
affect

ag-	*al-*	*ap-*
aggressive	allot	appear
aggravate	allow	apportion
aggrieved	alleviate	approach
		appoint

ar-	*as-*	*at-*
arrest	assign	attack
arrive	assemble	attend
arrange	assert	attention
		attract

Dictate words from the lists above for students to **spell**.

Closing

- **What are chameleon prefixes and why do you think they are called that?** (*prefixes in which the final letter of the prefix changes due to the first letter of the base element; like a chameleon lizard, they change depending on what they are next to*)

Follow-Up

- Have students complete the activities in Handout 4.3.

Handout

4.3 Latin Chameleon Prefixes

Reminder

Chameleon prefixes, often called *assimilated prefixes*, change the last letter of the prefix in order to alter the sound so the words can be said more easily.

Activities

1. Change the prefix *con-* to one of its variant forms (*col-*, *com-*, or *cor-*) as needed to make a familiar word. Write the prefix in the blank and the new word on the line.

   a. com + mute = commute

   b. cor + rupt = corrupt

   c. con + vince = convince

   d. col + lect = collect

   e. col + lide = collide

   f. con + form = conform

   g. cor + rode = corrode

   h. com + bine = combine

2. Choose a word above to complete the sentences below:

   a. Try to convince your classmates to attend the assembly.

   b. Combine the eggs, milk, and flour to make the pancake batter.

   c. Fortunately, the planes didn't collide in the air.

   d. The metal might corrode over a long time.

   e. Please collect the trash thrown from cars onto the roadway.

   f. His daily commute was 20 miles each way.

   g. The corrupt mayor was extremely annoyed at the charges.

3. Change the prefix *in-* to one of its variant forms (*il-*, *im-*, or *ir-*) as needed to make a familiar word. Write the prefix in the blank and the new word on the line.

   a. in + vite = invite

   b. ir + responsible = irresponsible

   c. ir + regular = irregular

Student Handout Answers

d. __il__ + legal = __illegal__

e. __im__ + portant = __important__

f. __in__ + formation = __information__

g. __ir__ + rigation = __irrigation__

h. __il__ + legible = __illegible__

4. Use words above to complete each sentence:

a. His handwriting was __illegible__.

b. He gave me __information__ on the cost of the new sailboat.

c. He was charged with __illegal__ breaking and entering.

d. __Invite__ your neighbors to the graduation party.

e. The __irrigation__ ditch was filled with water.

f. It was __irresponsible__ of him to forget the meeting.

g. Her __irregular__ heartbeat was cause for concern.

h. It was an __important__ decision on the judge's part.

5. Make a word with each variant form of the prefix *sub- (suc-, sug-, suf-,* and *sup-):*

a. ____________ b. ____________

c. ____________ d. ____________

6. Make a word with each variant form of the prefix *ad- (af-, ag-, al-, ap-, ar-, as-,* and *at-):*

a. ____________ b. ____________

c. ____________ d. ____________

e. ____________ f. ____________

g. ____________

7. Circle the words that contain chameleon prefixes in the following sentences:

a. The jury (succeeded) in (acquitting) the (corrupt) banker.

b. Her (appointment) frustrated the (aggressive) (attorney).

c. He (imported) the (supplies) (illegally).

d. She acted (irresponsibly) during the (committee) meeting.

e. The (irrigation) ditch provided (access) to the (compound).

f. The defense (suppressed) some (important) findings.

g. Police (arrested) the (aggressive) and (imbalanced) soldier.

h. Several drivers were (irritated) during their (commute) due to the nasty (collision).

Latin Suffixes

Opening

Today we are going to continue to break words apart to make them easier to read. We'll be talking about suffixes, or word endings, in this and the next lesson. Suffixes usually change the part of speech in a base word. When we add the suffix *-ed* to a verb, we know that it places the verb in the past tense. When we add the suffix *-s* to the end of nouns, the *s* means the noun is plural. We'll read and spell many words with Latin suffixes.

Objective

Students will learn about the common Latin suffixes. They will read and spell words containing these suffixes.

Procedure

Here are three lists of words. How are they the same? (all contain suffixes) What are the common parts? (suffixes) Where are these parts in the word? (at the end) Let's *read* these words.

List 1	*List 2*	*List 3*
generous	reality	difference
humorous	acuity	competence
tremendous	captivity	conference
nervous	ability	influence
oblivious	charity	belligerence
obvious	adversity	insistence
serious	dignity	persistence
mountainous	eternity	dependence

Most suffixes do not have specific meanings; rather, they give a word a particular part of speech. For example, words ending in *-ous* are adjectives, while *-ity, -ence,* and *-or* words are nouns. Many suffixes can be used in several parts of speech (e.g., *-age* in courage = a noun, but *-age* in manage = a verb).

In addition, most vowels in suffixes have schwa sounds, as the accent tends to be on the root word, not the suffix.

List other common Latin suffixes, and have students **generate** words for each pattern (see the examples listed below). Write the words on the board under each heading. Students should **read** and **spell** words from these lists.

-ist (noun, person)	***-ive*** (adjective)	***-age*** (noun/verb)	***-ant*** (noun/adjective)	***-ent*** (noun/adjective)
dentist	active	courage	abundant	coherent
scientist	additive	damage	defendant	absent
chemist	aggressive	salvage	elegant	dependent
flutist	cohesive	storage	entrant	competent
violinist	assertive	forage	observant	eminent
artist	digestive	marriage	tenant	resident
pianist	relative	pillage	defiant	fluent
biologist	sensitive	heritage	brilliant	independent

Here is another group of common suffixes, with examples. Ask students to **read** and **spell** words from the lists below.

-or (noun)	***-ar*** (adjective)	***-ible*** (adjective)	**Other Latin suffixes:**
actor	angular	edible	*-ary* (adjective/noun)
doctor	popular	incredible	*-ize* (verb)
editor	muscular	horrible	*-ance* (noun)
inspector	circular	impossible	*-t*(ure) (noun)
conductor	solar	visible	pasture
collector	lunar	audible	lecture
inventor	regular	terrible	picture
professor	insular	forcible	departure
translator	singular	destructible	nature
advisor	cellular	legible	adventure
donator	rectangular	reversible	fixture

Closing

- Review key concepts about these suffixes.

Follow-Up

- Have students complete the activities in Handout 4.4.

Handout

4.4 Latin Suffixes

Reminders

Suffixes are meaningful word parts that come at the end of words. There are numerous suffixes that are used mostly with Latin word roots. These suffixes place a base word into various parts of speech.

The vowels in suffixes generally contain the schwa sound.

Activities

1. Put the following words under the appropriate headings below (by part of speech):

generous	different	adversity
discourage	abundant	activity
realize	manage	novelist

Noun	Adjective	Verb
adversity	generous	discourage
activity	different	realize
novelist	abundant	manage

2. Circle the suffixes in the following words:

inventor	terrible	adventure	ignorant
popular	scientist	assertive	collector
stupidity	heritage	desolate	identify

3. Choose a word from the following list to make complete sentences below:

conference	obvious	adventurous	popular
editor	incredible	lecture	consecutive

a. The professor gave a forceful lecture.

b. Indiana Jones is an adventurous archaeologist.

c. We attended the literacy conference at the college.

d. The differences in the movies were obvious.

e. His technical ability was incredible.

f. The newspaper ___editor___ was well known in the city.

g. The ___popular___ song was sung by the children.

h. He missed three ___consecutive___ meetings.

4. Add suffixes to the base words. Write each new word on the line. Remember to use suffix addition rules when necessary.

a. conduct + or = ___conductor___

b. incred + ible = ___incredible___

c. translate + or = ___translator___

d. relate + ive = ___relative___

e. observe + ant = ___observant___

f. carry + age = ___carriage___

g. depart + ure = ___departure___

h. reverse + ible = ___reversible___

5. Write a sentence with each of the following words to show you know the word's meaning. You may use a dictionary.

oblivious ______________________________

____

persistence ______________________________

____

assertive ______________________________

____

abundant ______________________________

____

Latin Suffixes (/shən/) and More

Opening

There is another important set of suffixes from Latin. These include *-tion, -sion, -cian, -tious, -tial, -cial,* and *-cious.* The vowel digraphs in the suffix are all pronounced as schwa sounds. In addition, notice that all the initial consonants are pronounced like /sh/, as in *shut.* The consonants *c, t,* and *s* are often part of the root word.

Objective

Students will learn a variety of Latin suffixes containing *ci, si,* and *ti.*

Procedure

List the following suffixes on the board and have students generate words for each column (see examples shown below):

***-tion* /shən/**

vacation	nutrition
distraction	repetition
construction	superstition
subtraction	partition
addition	ignition
direction	notification
expedition	detention

***-sion* /shən/**

compression	pretension
depression	compulsion
expression	repulsion
impression	apprehension
progression	comprehension
confession	tension
admission	transmission

***-sion* /zhən/**

invasion	evasion
conclusion	erosion
exclusion	explosion
inclusion	confusion
preclusion	division
intrusion	revision
protrusion	aversion

***-cian* (person)**

magician	politician
musician	patrician
physician	mathematician
electrician	tactician
statistician	pediatrician

-tious	*-tial*	*-cial*	*-cious*
ambitious	initial	beneficial	vicious
nutritious	essential	crucial	delicious
expeditious	partial	official	malicious
repetitious	confidential	judicial	judicious
superstitious	celestial	facial	suspicious
fictitious	substantial	glacial	auspicious
scrumptious	differential	special	nutritious

Dictate a variety of words from the lists from the past two lessons or from other sources. Be sure students listen carefully for the suffix in each word. Additional words to dictate and have students **spell** include the following:

fraction	confusion	pertinent	realize
infection	explosion	mentally	refrigerator
connection	division	radiator	investigator
auction	automation	monitor	identity
notion	compatible	legislature	marvelous
portion	communicate	literature	ruinous

Closing

- Have students review Latin suffixes and how they are useful for reading and spelling.

Follow-Up

- Have students look for Latin suffixes in their social studies textbooks.
- Have students complete the activities in Handout 4.5.

Handout 4.5 Latin Suffixes (/shən/) and More

Reminders

Several important Latin suffixes contain *ci*, *si*, or *ti*, as in *facial*, *admission*, and *invention*.

The digraphs *ci*, *si*, and *ti* all have the sound /sh/ in these suffixes. You will notice they all come before a vowel in the suffix.

Activities

1. What are the ways to spell the suffix pronounced as /shən/?
   tion ______ sion ______ cian ______
2. What are the ways to spell the suffix pronounced as /shəl/?
   tial ______ cial ______
3. What is the way to spell the suffix pronounced as /zhən/?
   sion ______
4. What are the ways to spell the suffix pronounced as /shəs/?
   tious ______ cious ______
5. What is the way to spell the suffix /shən/ when used to signal that the word is a person?
   cian ______
6. Use the following words in a sentence.

   malicious ______________________________

   ____

   confidential ______________________________

   ____

   aversion ______________________________

   ____

   physician ______________________________

   ____

Lesson

4.6 Latin Roots (rupt, port, form, tract, scrib/scribe/script, spec/spect)

Opening

Today we're going to continue breaking words apart to make them easier to read and spell. We have been working on Latin prefixes and suffixes. For the next four lessons, we will talk about Latin root words.

Objective

Students will learn common Latin word roots and their meanings. They will read and spell words containing these roots.

Procedure

Who knows what a root word is? (*the main part of a word; the part to which prefixes and suffixes are added; the root usually receives the accent or stress in Latin-based words*) **Roots are valuable not only as patterns for decoding and spelling, but also for learning new vocabulary to enhance your reading, writing, listening, and speaking, since each root has a specific meaning.**

Begin by writing *rupt* on the board. Ask students to **generate** a number of words with *rupt* as the root (see examples below). Write these words on the board. See if students can guess the meaning of *rupt* (to break, to burst) based on the words on the board.

rupt
rupture
erupt
eruption
corrupt
bankrupt
abruptly
interruption
disruptive
irrupt
interrupted

For each group of words, have students recognize the common parts (the roots). Have them note the placement of the root (the beginning if there is no prefix, the end if there is no suffix, the middle if there are prefixes and suffixes).

NOTE: The words listed are only a few of the many possible words. Additional suffixes may be added to most of the following words. Notice, also, that some roots have more than one form.

port **(to carry)**		***form*** **(to shape)**		***tract*** **(to pull)**	
import	imported	reform	informal	tractor	subtract
export	exporting	deform	informative	traction	retract
portable	exportable	inform	information	attract	attractive
transport	transportation	transform	transforming	distract	distraction
porter	deport	conform	conformed	extract	extraction
deportation	support	formula	formal	contract	contractual
supportive	supports	misinform	uniform	intractable	contractor
reporter	insupportable	perform	informant	distractible	abstract

scrib, scribe, script **(to write)**		***spec, spect*** **(to see, to watch)**	
scribble	prescribe	spectator	respect
ascribe	prescription	spectacle	respectful
describe	scripture	spectacular	disrespect
description	transcript	species	disrespectful
inscribe	descriptive	special	perspective
inscription	circumscribe	specimen	retrospective
manuscript	nondescript	speculator	prospector

Select 5 to 10 words above for students to **spell** from dictation.

Closing

- **What did we study today?** (*Latin word roots*)
- **Why are these word parts important?** (*helpful units to recognize for decoding and spelling and to gain meaning from longer words*)

Follow-Up

- Have students write one root (with its forms) on separate pages of their notebook. Ask them to find additional words to add to their lists. Encourage students to use readers, literature, textbooks, dictionaries, or any other sources (including family members or friends) to find additional words.
- Have students complete the activities in Handout 4.6.

Handout 4.6 Latin Roots (rupt, port, form, tract, scrib/scribe/script, spec/spect)

Reminder

Latin word roots are important morphemes, or meaning units. Each Latin word root has a specific meaning, so when they are learned, these word roots provide an efficient way to read, spell, and gain meaning from words.

Activities

1. Match the root with the letter of its meaning:

b. rupt	a. to see, to watch
e. port	b. to break, to burst
d. form	c. to pull
f. scrib, scribe, script	d. to shape
a. spec, spect	e. to carry
c. tract	f. to write

2. Use the following words to complete each sentence below:

portable	misinformation	manuscript	spectacular
attractive	ruptured	retrospect	erupted

a. The attorney gave his client misinformation about the accident.

b. Portable radios are useful in times of earthquakes and tornadoes.

c. The attractive garden left the tourists with many memories.

d. The Hawaiian volcano erupted with spectacular force.

e. Turn your manuscript in on Thursday.

f. His appendix ruptured during his gym class.

g. We saw things differently, in retrospect.

3. Circle the prefixes, underline the Latin roots, and circle the suffixes in the following words. (There may be more than one prefix and suffix in a word.)

interruption	disinformation	inscription	inspector
respectfully 	informal	deported	disruptive
prescribes	extraction	disrespectful	transporting

Latin Roots (stru/struct, dic/dict, flect/flex, mit/miss)

Opening

Today we'll continue learning new Latin root words. Who remembers some of the roots we talked about in the last lesson? Remember that words containing Latin word roots often appear in your literature, social studies, and science books. Review the Latin roots from Lesson 4.6.

Objective

Students will learn four new Latin word roots and their meanings. They will read and spell words containing these roots.

Procedure

Begin by writing the new Latin roots listed below on the board. Ask students to **generate** a number of words with these roots. Write these words on the board. See if students can pick up the meaning of the roots from the words on the board. Next, have students review by **reading** all words.

NOTE: These four Latin roots have two forms. Be sure to point this out to your students.

stru, struct **(to build)**

structure	instruct
structural	instructor
construct	instructive
construction	obstruct
reconstruction	instrument
reconstructionist	destructive
infrastructure	superstructure

dic, dict **(to say, to tell)**

dictate	dictation
dictator	dictum
dictaphone	contradict
predict	edict
prediction	indicate
diction	malediction
predicament	benediction

flect, flex **(to bend)**

flex	genuflect
flexible	circumflex
inflexible	reflector
deflect	deflection
inflection	reflect
reflex	reflexes
flexibility	inflexible

mit, miss **(to send)**

mission	dismiss
missile	intermission
missive	remiss
admit	remit
admission	permit
commit	submit
commission	transmit

Ask students to **spell** some of the words above as you dictate them. They can also **spell** sentences such as the following:

- His flexibility was well known.
- She transmitted the message.
- Try not to contradict your teacher.

Closing

- **Who remembers why it's important to learn the common Latin word roots?** (*the roots are word parts found in many words; they help not only reading and spelling but vocabulary as well*)

Follow-Up

- Have students complete the activities in Handout 4.7.

Handout 4.7 Latin Roots (stru/struct, dic/dict, flect/flex, mit/miss)

Reminder

Roots often have more than one form. In this lesson, each of the new roots had two forms. You learned earlier that the Latin root meaning "to write" has three forms (*scrib, scribe, script*).

Activities

1. Match the root with the letter of its meaning.

h.	stru, struct	a. to write
f.	dic, dict	b. to send
j.	flect, flex	c. to see, to watch
b.	mit, miss	d. to carry
i.	rupt	e. to shape
d.	port	f. to say, to tell
e.	form	g. to pull
g.	tract	h. to build
a.	scrib, scribe, script	i. to break, to burst
c.	spec, spect	j. to bend

2. Use the following words to complete each sentence below:

reflector	intermission	committee	dictator
instructor	destructive	predicted	submitted

a. She submitted the bill to her client.

b. Instructor is another word for teacher or professor.

c. The reflector on his bicycle broke yesterday.

d. We went out for popcorn and drinks during intermission.

e. The finance committee met during the lunch hour.

f. Sunday's destructive winds were not predicted by the meteorologist.

g. Fidel Castro was a dictator in Cuba until February 2008.

3. List the part of speech (verb, noun, adjective) for the words in each row:

a. admission, intermission, dictator, instrument, reflector Noun

b. obstruct, predict, indicate, remit, transmit, instruct Verb

c. destructive, respectful, distractible, portable Adjective

Latin Roots (cred, duc/duce/duct, pel/puls, pend/pens, fac/fact/fec, vert/vers, ject)

Opening

Today we will study an additional seven new Latin root words. These roots are found in hundreds of words.

Objective

Students will learn seven new Latin roots and their meanings. They will read and spell words and discuss the meaning of unfamiliar words.

Procedure

Begin by writing the new Latin roots listed below on the board. Ask students to **generate** a number of words with these roots. Write these words on the board. See if students can pick up the meaning of the roots from the words on the board. Next, have students review by **reading** all words.

NOTE: Most of these roots have two or three forms. Be sure to point this out to your students.

cred **(to believe)**

credit	credential
discredit	credible
accredit	incredible
creditor	credulous
accreditation	incredulous
credulity	credence

duc, duce, duct **(to lead)**

conduct	educate
deduct	education
deduce	induce
introduce	produce
reduce	reduction
aqueduct	productive

pel, puls **(to drive, to push)**

impel	impulse
compel	compulsion
expel	expulsion
propel	propulsion
dispel	impulsive
compulsory	repellent

pend, pens **(to hang, to weigh)**

pending	pendant
pendulum	dependent
dependability	independent
interdependent	suspend
pensive	suspense
expensive	compensate

***fac, fact, fec* (to make, to do)**

fact	faculty
facile	facility
manufacture	facilitate
factory	satisfaction
affect	affection
disinfectant	effective

***vert, vers* (to turn)**

convert	conversion
convertible	versus
introvert	extrovert
divert	diversion
avert	aversion
revert	reversible

***ject* (to throw, to lie)**

deject	dejected	dejection	adjective
reject	rejected	rejection	conjecture
object	objective	objection	objectivity
eject	ejection	inject	injection
project	projection	projectile	projector
interject	projectionist	trajectory	

Dictate a variety of these words for students to **spell**. Have students **identify** the root in each word before they **write** the word. For additional **spelling** practice, dictate some of the words in sentences for students to **write** the entire sentence.

Closing

- **What parts of words have we been studying? Why is this useful?** (*Latin roots; recognizing these word parts helps us read and spell words and understand word meanings*)

Follow-Up

- Have students find new words containing the Latin roots from this and the past two lessons.
- Have students add the new roots with examples to their notebooks.
- Have students complete the activities in Handout 4.8.

Handout

4.8 Latin Roots (cred, duc/duce/duct, pel/puls, pend/pens, fac/fact/fec, vert/vers, ject)

Reminder

You were introduced to seven new Latin word roots: These are *cred, duc/duce/duct, pel/puls, pend/pens, fac/fact/fec, vert/vers,* and *ject.*

Activities

1. Match the letter of the correct meaning with the root:

d. cred	a. to hang, to weigh
g. duc, duce, duct	b. to turn
e. pel, puls	c. to make, to do
a. pend, pens	d. to believe
c. fac, fact, fec	e. to drive, to push
b. vert, vers	f. to throw, to lie
f. ject	g. to lead

2. Use the following words to complete each sentence:

educator	credentials	impulsive	pendulum
vertigo	manufacturer	projector	effective

a. The high school educator taught history for 30 years.
b. The manufacturer of the expensive computers went bankrupt.
c. He bought a new projector with the birthday check.
d. The senator waged an effective campaign.
e. The clock's pendulum swung back and forth all day and night.
f. Charlie's vertigo was especially bad at extreme heights.
g. Maria's impulsive behavior disturbed her friends.
h. The professor held outstanding credentials from Stanford University.

3. List the part of speech (verb, noun, adjective) for the words in each row:
a. reversed, manufacture, disinfect, expend Verb
b. compulsive, credible, pensive, affectionate Adjective
c. credential, educator, projection, conductor Noun

Latin Roots (fer, ven/vent, vid/vis, aud)

Opening

Today we will continue to learn about Latin roots. This will be our final lesson on Latin roots before we move on to the Greek combining forms.

Objective

Students will study an additional four Latin roots. They will read and spell words and discuss the meaning of words containing these roots.

Procedure

Begin by writing the new Latin roots listed below on the board. Ask students to **generate** a number of words with these roots (see example words below). Write these words on the board. See if students can pick up the meaning of the roots from the words written on the board. Next, have students review by **reading** all the words generated.

fer **(to bear, to yield)**

refer	confer	differ
reference	conferring	difference
offer	offering	defer
deference	fertile	fertilizer
coniferous	suffer	insufferable
prefer	preferable	transfer
transferal	vociferous	referendum

NOTE: Words containing the root *fer* don't always follow traditional suffix addition rules. For example, *offer, suffer,* and *differ* never double the final *r,* no matter what suffix is added (e.g., *offering, suffered, different*). Other *fer* words do double, but only with the suffixes *-ed, -ing,* and *-al* (e.g., *conferred, transferring, referral*).

ven, vent **(to come)**

convene	convention	advent
adventure	adventurer	circumvent
contravene	event	eventual
invent	invention	inventor
intervene	intervention	misadventure
prevent	prevented	preventable
preventive	unconventional	uneventful
venture	venturesome	covenant

***vid, vis* (to see)**

advise	advisor	provide
provision	providence	visual
visualization	visualize	revise
revision	supervise	supervisor
televise	television	visible
invisible	visitation	indivisible
improvise	improvisation	evidence
evident	divide	division

***aud* (to hear, to listen)**

audio	audience	audible
audibility	audit	audition
auditorium	inaudible	subaudible
audiometer	audiology	audiologist
audiogram	audiovisual	auditor

Dictate the following sentences for students to **spell**:

- The audience enjoyed the spectacular audiovisual presentation.
- The convention provided new information for the conferees.

Closing

- **Why is it useful to learn specific Latin word roots?** (*to help read, spell, and understand the meaning of unfamiliar words*)

Follow-Up

- Have students complete the activities in Handout 4.9.

Handout

4.9 Latin Roots (*fer, ven/vent, vid/vis, aud*)

Reminder

Four new roots were introduced in Lesson 4.9: *fer, ven/vent, vid/vis,* and *aud.*

Activities

1. Match the letter of the correct meaning with the root.

d. fer	a. to come
a. ven, vent	b. to see
b. vid, vis	c. to hear
c. aud	d. to bear, to yield

2. Use the following words to complete each sentence:

transfer	convention	television	auditorium
video games	audience	referred	prevent

a. Please transfer the books to the trunk of my car.

b. His favorite television show was *Star Trek*.

c. The audience enjoyed the Bruce Springsteen concert.

d. We attended the reading convention in Seattle.

e. The principal referred the ill student to the school nurse.

f. I like most of the video games at the mall.

g. Smoky the Bear asks us to prevent forest fires.

3. List the part of speech (verb, noun, adjective) for the words in each row:

a. referral, conference, audition, television Noun

b. preventable, visual, fertile, audible Adjective

c. prevent, offer, advise, fertilize Verb

Lesson 4.10 Greek Combining Forms (34 Common Forms)

Opening

Today we will switch from words of Latin origin to words of Greek origin. You may remember that these words are often used in science and math classes and textbooks.

Different people use different terms to describe the Greek word parts. In some dictionaries and books, they are called *roots;* in some they become *combining forms;* in others they are known as *prefixes* and *suffixes.* In this manual, they will be called *combining forms,* as usually there are two parts of equal stress and importance that are combined, almost as in Anglo-Saxon compound words. Some of the parts come only at the beginning of a word, and others come only at the end. Some forms can be used in either position.

Objective

Students will review Greek letter-sound correspondences and learn about Greek combining forms. They will read and spell words containing Greek word parts.

Procedure

On the board, **write** word parts that usually come at the beginning of words and then write those that usually come at the end of words.

Beginning

auto	arch	meta
phono	phys	theo
photo	psych	metro
biblio	micro	mono
hydro	peri	philo
hyper	bi	soph
tele	semi	techni
chron	hemi	
chrom	mega	

End

graph	ology	sphere
gram	polis	crat
meter	cracy	scope

NOTE: Alert students to the Greek letter-sound correspondences that are prevalent in these combining forms (as studied in Unit 2—e.g., *ch, ph, y* as medial vowel, and silent *p* as in *pn, ps,* and *pt,* among others, like *rh* and *mn*).

Have students use the Greek word parts above to **generate** words such as these:

chronometer	perimeter	microscope
physiology	physician	periscope
bibliography	physiologist	telescope
telegraph	metropolis	architect
autobiography	zoology	autograph
hyperactive	metropolitan	archeology
phonograph	hemisphere	hydrogen
philosophy	philharmonic	theology

Dictate a number of words (such as those listed above) with Greek word parts for students to **spell**.

Closing

- Review the terminology and origin of the Greek combining forms taught in this lesson.
- Let students know that in the next lesson, they will deal with the specific meaning of many of these Greek combining forms.

Follow-Up

- Have students complete the activities in Handout 4.10.

Handout

4.10 Greek Combining Forms (34 Common Forms)

Reminders

Words of Greek origin are used frequently in the fields of math and science.

Many Greek combining forms contain unique letter-sound correspondences, such as *ph* /f/ *(photograph)*, *ch* /k/ *(chronometer)*, *y* /ĭ/ or /ī/ *(symphony; hydroplane)*, *mn* /n/ *(mnemonic)*, *pn* /n/ *(pneumonia)*, *rh* /r/ *(rhinoceros)*, *ps* /s/ *(psychiatry)*, and *pt* /t/ *(pterodactyl)*.

Activities

1. Circle the unique letter-sound correspondences in the following words. Try to read the words.

chlorophyll	photograph	symphony	hydrogen
synchronize	pneumatic	psychologist	mnemonics
rhythmic	pteropod	astrophysics	photosynthesis

2. Divide the following Greek-based words into syllables. You can use a dictionary.

pho|to|graph	mi|cro|scope	der|ma|to|lo|gy
bib|li|og|ra|phy	mon|o|logue	ther|mom|e|ter
me|ga|pod	tech|no|crat	hy|po|der|mic

3. Make words using as many of the following Greek combining forms as you can.

tele	photo	phono	graph
gram	meter	hypo	chron
poly	psych	ology	sphere
hemi	scope	auto	micro

a. ____________________ b. ____________________

c. ____________________ d. ____________________

e. ____________________ f. ____________________

g. ____________________ h. ____________________

i. ____________________ j. ____________________

k. ____________________ l. ____________________

m. ____________________ n. ____________________

o. ____________________ p. ____________________

Greek Combining Forms (*phon/phono, photo, graph/gram, auto, tele, log/ology*)

Opening

Today we'll discuss six specific Greek forms and their meanings. We'll read and spell many words containing these combining forms.

Objective

Students will learn six common Greek combining forms. They will read and spell words containing these word parts, as well as discuss the meaning of each form.

Procedure

Write the following Greek combining forms on the board:

phon, phono (sound)	*auto* (self)
photo (light)	*tele* (distant)
graph, gram (written/drawn)	*ology* (study)

See if students can **generate** words containing these forms (see example words below). Discuss the meaning of the words students provide. Then have students **read** the words.

phon, phono

phone	phonics	phoneme
phonograph	phonology	phonogram

photo

photocopy	photoflash	photographer

graph, gram

graphics	graphite	photograph
photography	autograph	photogram

auto

automation	automatic	automobile

tele

telecast	telegram	telegraph
telephone	telephoto	telethon

Dictate the following sentences for your students to **spell**:

- The instructor took the photograph.
- The dictator telegraphed the photographer.
- Our automobile was pulled by the tractor.

Closing

- **What did we study today?** (*Greek combining forms*)
- **Why is it useful to learn these combining forms?** (*because they appear in thousands of words; helpful for reading, spelling, and gaining meaning*)

Follow-Up

- Hold a contest. Place students in small groups. See which group can find the most words of Greek origin in their science textbooks. Students may challenge other group decisions.
- Have students complete the activities in Handout 4.11.

Handout

4.11 Greek Combining Forms (*phon/phono, photo, graph/gram, auto, tele, log/ology*)

Reminder

You learned six specific Greek combining forms and their meanings: *phon/phono, photo, graph/gram, auto, tele,* and *log/ology.*

Activities

1. Match the letter of the correct meaning with the root:

d.	phon/phono	a. self
c.	photo	b. distant
f.	graph/gram	c. light
a.	auto	d. sound
b.	tele	e. study
e.	ology	f. written, drawn

2. Use the following words to complete each sentence below:

autograph	phonology	photography	telephone
telegram	telethon	phonograph	autobiography

a. Former President Clinton wrote an interesting autobiography.

b. He signed his autograph on the front page for me.

c. Phonology is the study of speech sounds.

d. Prior to CDs, DVDs, and iPods, we listened to music on a phonograph.

e. Mother interrupted me while I was on the telephone with my friend.

f. In the past, good and bad news was often sent by telegram.

g. I studied photography in high school and took some excellent pictures.

h. My dad often participated in the telethon for muscular dystrophy.

Lesson

4.12 Greek Combining Forms (*micro, meter, therm, bio, scope, hydro*)

Opening

Today we'll discuss six more specific Greek forms and their meanings. We'll read and spell many words.

Objective

Students will learn six additional Greek combining forms. They will read and spell words containing these word parts, as well as discuss the meaning of each form.

Procedure

Write the following Greek combining forms on the board:

micro (small)	bio (life)
meter (measure)	scope (watch, see)
therm (heat)	hydro (water)

See if students can **generate** words containing the forms above. Discuss the meaning of the words students generate. (Below is a sample of words that might be generated.)

micro

microscope microgram microphone micrometer

meter

barometer speedometer pedometer audiometer

therm

thermal thermodynamics thermostat thermometer

bio

biology biography autobiography autobiographical

scope

telescope hydroscope microscope periscope

hydro

hydrogen hydrophone hydrostat hydroelectric

Dictate the following sentences for students to **spell**:

- The biologist wrote his biography.
- The instructor used a microphone.
- The telescopic lens caught the volcano's eruption.
- Set the thermometer to a comfortable temperature.

Closing

- **What parts of words did we study today?** (*Greek combining forms*)
- **Why is it useful to learn these combining forms?** (*because they appear in thousands of words and are helpful for both reading and spelling*)

Follow-Up

- Ask students to look for Greek combining forms in their math and science textbooks.
- Have students complete the activities in Handout 4.12.

Handout

4.12 Greek Combining Forms (*micro, meter, therm, bio, scope, hydro*)

Reminder

You learned six new Greek combining forms in Lesson 4.12: *micro, meter, therm, bio, scope,* and *hydro.*

Activities

1. Match the root to the letter of the correct meaning.

d. micro	a. to watch, to see
e. meter	b. heat
b. therm	c. water
f. bio	d. small
a. scope	e. measure
c. hydro	f. life

2. Use the following words to complete each sentence below:

hydroelectric	microscope	telescope	thermometer
biography	autobiography	thermostat	perimeter

a. He wrote his autobiography when he retired from the U.S. Senate.

b. The astronomer looked at stars through a telescope .

c. The physician looked at cells through a microscope .

d. The Hoover Dam produced large amounts of hydroelectric power.

e. Mother always turned up the thermostat when she was cold.

f. We measured the perimeter of the property.

g. We need a new thermometer to measure the lake temperatures.

h. Many authors have written biographies about Abraham Lincoln.

Lesson 4.13 Greek Combining Forms (*biblio, crat/cracy, geo, metro, pol/polis, dem*)

Opening

Today we'll discuss six more specific Greek forms and their meanings. We'll read and spell many words.

Objective

Students will learn six additional Greek combining forms. They will read and spell words containing these word parts, as well as discuss the meaning of each form.

Procedure

Write the following Greek combining forms on the board:

biblio (book)	metro (mother city, measure)
crat, cracy (rule)	pol/polis (city, method of government)
geo (earth)	dem (people)

See if students can **generate** words containing these forms. Discuss the meaning of the words students generate. (See a sample of words that might be generated below.)

biblio

bibliography	bibliographer	bibliophile

crat, cracy

democrat	autocratic	democracy
aristocrat	aristocracy	

geo

geology	geologist	geopolitics
geography	geometry	

metro

metropolitan	metropolis	metronome

pol/polis

police	political	cosmopolitan
politician	Minneapolis	metropolis

dem

demographics demagog epidemic

Dictate the following sentences for your students to **spell**:

- The large metropolis was led by the democratic mayor.
- She was a well-known photographer and geologist.
- The bibliography included many political decisions.

Closing

- **What parts of words did we study today?** (*Greek combining forms*)
- **Why is it useful to learn these combining forms?** (*because they appear in thousands of words and are helpful for both reading and spelling*)

Follow-Up

- Ask students to look for more Greek combining forms in their math and science textbooks.
- Have students complete the activities in Handout 4.13.

NOTE: You may also want to present the Greek numbers. See the Assorted Word Lists section of this manual for both Latin and Greek prefixes and combining forms expressing numbers.

Handout

4.13 Greek Combining Forms (*biblio, crat/cracy, geo, metro, pol/polis, dem*)

Reminder

In Lesson 4.13, you learned six new Greek combining forms: *biblio, crat/cracy, geo, metro, pol/polis,* and *dem.*

Activities

1. Match the root to the letter of the correct meaning.

__d.__ biblio	a. people
__c.__ crat, cracy	b. mother city, measure
__f.__ geo	c. rule
__b.__ metro	d. book
__e.__ pol/polis	e. city, method of government
__a.__ dem	f. earth

2. Use the following words to complete each sentence below:

geologist	Minneapolis	bibliophiles	bibliographer
democratic	metropolitan	geography	metronome

a. The __bibliographer__ enjoyed writing about the lives of famous people.

b. We have a __democratic__ form of government in the United States.

c. The famous __geologist__ studied rock formations on the East coast.

d. My favorite subject is __geography__.

e. I use a __metronome__ to keep time while I practice my scales on the piano.

f. __Bibliophiles__ absolutely love books.

g. __Minneapolis__ is an important __metropolitan__ city.

Lesson 4.14 Review of Morpheme Patterns

Opening

Today we will review the word parts we have studied in this unit. We will read words and try to identify the origin of the word.

Objective

Students will review the word parts they have learned. They will read and spell words and try to identify word origin.

Procedure

Who remembers the three layers of the language we have been studying? (*Anglo-Saxon, Latin, and Greek*)

What meaning units, or morphemes, have we studied? (*prefixes, suffixes, roots, Greek combining forms; Anglo-Saxon compound words studied in Unit 3*)

Write the following words on the board:

reconstruction	flashlight	archeology
conductor	subjective	reflection
hemisphere	eating	revision
semicircle	underhanded	undress
cowbell	autocracy	pretending
reflection	graphics	physical
autograph	spectacular	railroad

Have students **read** the words aloud. Ask students to tell you word origin. They should provide a rationale for the choice of origin (e.g., *common Latin suffix -tion; Greek because of the ph; Anglo-Saxon*).

Have students identify the important word parts.

Closing

- Review with students the purpose for identifying prefixes, roots, and suffixes in words.

Follow-Up

- Have students complete the activities in Handout 4.14.
- Administer the Unit 4 Quiz found on the CD.

Handout

4.14 Review of Morpheme Patterns

Reminders

You have learned numerous morphemes from Anglo-Saxon, Latin, and Greek during this unit. Remember that morphemes help us in reading, spelling, and understanding the meaning of numerous words.

The morphemes may be grouped as follows:

- Base words
- Compound words
- Prefixes
- Suffixes
- Latin roots
- Greek combining forms (or roots)

Activities

1. The following words are from an article on prehistoric animals. See if you can identify the word origin for each of the words below.

turf	paleoarchaeology	pterodactyl	volcano
imprint	spearhead	anthropology	minerals
culture	tar pit	Stone Age	dinosaur
hunter	extinct	segregation	archaeology
earthquake	ancestors	aggregate	evolution
technology	geologist	paleontologist	toolmaker

2. Write the words in the appropriate column of word origin:

Anglo-Saxon	Latin	Greek
turf	volcano	paleoarchaeology
imprint	minerals	pterodactyl
spearhead	culture	anthropology
tar pit	extinct	dinosaur
Stone Age	segregation	archaeology
hunter	ancestors	technology
earthquake	aggregate	geologist
toolmaker	evolution	paleontologist

Unit

5 Strategies for Decoding and Spelling Long, Unfamiliar Words

Lessons

5.1 Introduction to Strategies for Decoding and Spelling Long, Unfamiliar Words

5.2 Decoding Long Words (Practice 1)

5.3 Decoding Long Words (Practice 2)

5.4 Spelling Long Words (Practice 1)

5.5 Spelling Long Words (Practice 2)

5.6 Spelling Rules for One-Syllable Words

5.7 Spelling Rules for Adding Suffixes (Final *e*)

5.8 Spelling Rules for Adding Suffixes (Doubling Rule)

5.9 Spelling Rules for Adding Suffixes (Final *y*)

5.10 Practice for Rule-Based Words

5.11 Review of Strategies for Decoding and Spelling Long, Unfamiliar Words

Introduction to Strategies for Decoding and Spelling Long, Unfamiliar Words

We have been studying many ways to analyze long, unfamiliar words. We have talked about phonics, or letter-sound correspondences; syllable patterns; and morphemes, or meaning parts of words—all patterns within the three layers of language: Anglo-Saxon, Latin, and Greek.

In this final unit, we will put all this information together so you can read and spell words more efficiently. We will talk about a sequence for using the strategies you have been learning. We'll continue to read and spell many words.

Opening

Today we're going to practice strategies for decoding (that is, reading) long, unfamiliar words. Researchers who study reading found that most fluent readers look first for morpheme patterns, then at possible places in a word to divide syllables, and last at letter-sound correspondences. Here is the decision process we will follow if you can't figure out the word from its context:

1. See if you can identify the word's language origin.
2. Look for the morpheme units: Anglo-Saxon or Latin prefixes, roots, suffixes, Greek combining forms, or single words making up Anglo-Saxon compound words.
3. If you can't find a morpheme—or if you find morphemes, but still can't read the word—try to break the word into syllables using the common syllable division options.
4. If syllable division doesn't work, or works for only part of the word, use letter-sound correspondences.

Write the following words on the board (or make copies for each student), and have students practice reading these words. Direct students in using the four-step process described above. (Give each student at least one word to try individually.) You may want students to analyze the words at the board so they can point out morphemes, syllables, and other patterns.

NOTE: List 1 is taken from third-grade texts and List 2 from fifth- and sixth-grade texts.

List 1	List 2
pretending	incongruous
understandable	superstitious
prevention	accumulation
reduction	hippopotamus
thunderhead	illustrious
dangerous	corruptible
boisterous	flamboyant
surrounding	boisterous
exclusive	maladroit
government	moisture
consideration	cantankerous
reconstructionist	semaphore
autograph	ophthalmoscope
disturbance	ambulatory
devotion	acquaintance
moisture	extraordinary
memorandum	pejorative
gymnasium	calumniously
incredible	euphemism

NOTE: Remember that for this activity, meaning of the terms is not important. You are giving students the opportunity to practice strategies for analyzing any number of words that may appear in their school or recreational reading.

Closing

- Review the four-step process for decoding long, unfamiliar words.
- Discuss why this process is useful. (It is the way very good readers seem to approach new and unfamiliar words.)

Follow-Up

- Give students a piece of text slightly above their reading level. Ask them to read the selection and practice reading new words using the four-step process above. (If you can give students markable passages—perhaps from *Junior Scholastic, Weekly Reader,* etc.—students can underline the difficult words. These can become a word bank for future decoding discussions.)
- Have students complete the activities in Handout 5.1.

Handout 5.1 Introduction to Strategies for Decoding and Spelling Long, Unfamiliar Words

Reminder

This final unit allows us to practice our new strategies and to review some of the patterns and rules we have studied. You learned that in order to read longer, unfamiliar words, it is helpful to use the following four-step procedure:

1. See if you can identify the language origin.
2. Look for the morpheme units: Anglo-Saxon or Latin prefixes, roots, suffixes, Greek combining forms, or single words making up Anglo-Saxon compound words.
3. If you can't find a morpheme—or if you find morphemes, but still can't read the word—try to break the word into syllables using the common syllable-division options.
4. If syllable division doesn't work, or works for only part of the word, use letter-sound correspondences.

Activities

1. First, identify the origin of each word listed below and write it on the first line. Second, look for morphemes or break the words into syllables; count the number of syllables in each word and write it on the second line. Then, read each word.

excursion		intensity		important	
L	3	L	4	L	3
memorandum		**desegregation**		**overwhelmingly**	
L	4	L	5	A-S	5
thermometer		**misanthropist**		**hydrosphere**	
Gk	4	Gk	4	Gk	3
vivacious		**appendectomy**		**sophisticated**	
L	3	L	5	Gk	5

2. Using some of the words above, complete each sentence below:

   a. I sent an ___important___ ___memorandum___ to the principal.

   b. My colorful and ___vivacious___ friend was liked ___overwhelmingly___.

Student Handout Answers

c. She was extremely ill prior to her __appendectomy__.

d. The __intensity__ of the course caused great anxiety.

e. The __hydrosphere__ refers to the waters of the earth.

f. Most of the students applauded the __desegregation__ order.

3. Read the following word: *malediction.*

a. What is the prefix? __male, or mal__

b. What is the root? __dict__

c. What is the suffix? __tion, or ion__

d. What is the language origin? __Latin__

e. How do you know? __root with affixes, polysyllabic__

f. What do you think is the meaning? ______

g. Look up the meaning in the dictionary: __1) A curse, 2) Slander__

Lesson

5.2 Decoding Long Words (Practice 1)

Opening

Today we're going to read numerous long words and see if we can apply the strategies we learned in the last lesson.

Objective

Students will practice reading long, unfamiliar words using the four-step strategy learned in the previous lesson.

Procedure

During the last decoding lesson, we learned how to "attack" long, unfamiliar words. We talked about strategies for reading long words. Who remembers the four steps in reading a long, unfamiliar word? (*(1) identify the language origin; (2) look for the morpheme units: Anglo-Saxon or Latin prefixes, roots, suffixes, Greek combining forms, or single words making up Anglo-Saxon compound words; (3) if you can't find a morpheme—or if you find morphemes, but still can't read the word—try to break the word into syllables using the common syllable division options; (4) if syllable division doesn't work, or works for only part of the word, use letter-sound correspondences*)

NOTE: Many of these words come from junior high school and high school science and social studies texts. You may want to add some words from the students' reading program, literature, and/or content area texts that you think will be problematic for decoding. You won't have time to go through all of these in one lesson. You will also want to use some of these words for spelling in the lessons that follow.

Have students **read** the following words, looking first for morphemes, next for syllables, and finally for letter-sound correspondences. These words are included in the Assorted Word Lists section of this manual.

Science Words	Social Studies Words
spontaneous	bicentennial
microorganism	guaranteed
electromagnetism	legislation
abiogenesis	unrealistic
clarification	colonization

galvanometer
investigation
imaginary
experiment
frequency
infrared
ultraviolet
spectrum
photosynthesis

essentially
hierarchy
proletariat
argumentative
sequential
ideology
oppressor
communism
socialism

Have students **spell** several of the words listed above.

Closing

- **How are these strategies useful in analyzing long, unfamiliar words?** (*it's useful to begin looking for familiar morphemes, then break into syllables, and finally use letter-sound correspondences for small pieces of the words*)

Follow-Up

- Have students practice using these strategies when they come to unfamiliar, long words.
- Have students complete the activities in Handout 5.2.

Handout
5.2 Decoding Long Words (Practice 1)

Reminder

Use the following steps in figuring out how to read long, unfamiliar words:

1. Identify the language origin.
2. Look for the morpheme units: Anglo-Saxon or Latin prefixes, roots, suffixes, Greek combining forms, or single words making up Anglo-Saxon compound words.
3. If you can't find a morpheme—or if you find morphemes, but still can't read the word—try to break the word into syllables using the common syllable-division options.
4. If syllable division doesn't work, or works for only part of the word, use letter-sound correspondences.

Activities

1. First, identify the origin of each word listed below and write it on the first line. Second, look for morphemes or break the words into syllables; count the number of syllables in each word and write it on the second line. Then, read each word.

Word	Origin	Syllables	Word	Origin	Syllables	Word	Origin	Syllables
illiterate	L	4	compromise	L	3	bibliomania	Gk	6
dyslexia	Gk	4	convergent	L	3	anthropologist	Gk	5
extraordinary	L	6	revolutionary	L	6	chronophobia	Gk	5
thermodynamics	Gk	5	megacycle	Gk	4	personification	L	6

2. Using some of the words above, complete each sentence below:

a. A ___megacycle___ refers to one million cycles.

b. The ___extraordinary___ ___anthropologist___ had ___revolutionary___ ideas about the origins of man.

c. ___Thermodynamics___ is the field that studies the relationships between heat and other forms of energy.

d. Persons with ___dyslexia___ need not be ___illiterate___.

3. Read the following word: *geothermal.*

a. Is there a prefix? ___No___

b. Is there a suffix? ___Yes___

c. List the combining forms: ___geo___ ___therm___

d. What is the language origin? ___Greek___

e. How do you know? ___Scientific, contains combining forms___

f. What do you think is the meaning? ______

g. Look up the meaning in the dictionary: ___Pertaining to the internal heat of the earth___

Lesson

5.3 Decoding Long Words (Practice 2)

Opening

Today we'll continue to read and spell more words from your content area texts.

Review the four-step process. Have students **read** some of the following words and **spell** some from dictation.

Science Words

assumption	ionization	molecular	activation
catalysts	reactants	subcutaneous	subterranean
visceral	extensibility	tendonitis	archaeology
illumination	intelligence	neurosurgeon	nitrogenous
myofilaments	hemodialysis	vertebrates	erythrocytes
fibrinogen	epidermis	zoologist	experimental
laboratory	hypotheses	behavioral	variable
theoretical	spectroheliograph	orthodontist	momentum
physics	chemistry	illuminate	spatiotemporal

Social Studies Words

perpetuate	dictatorship	peasants	dogma
caricature	elaborately	judicial	executive
presidential	electoral	columnists	politicians
reconstruction	secession	perpetuate	hieroglyph
surveillance	inalienable	Renaissance	isolationism
ambassador	subjugation	enlightenment	mummification
papyrus	mythology	multiculturalism	jurisdiction
monarchy	proclamation	naturalization	parasympathetic

Math Words

mathematician	statistics	dividend	quadrangle
bilateral	calculus	polygon	probability
quotient	estimate	simultaneous	computation
binomial	symbols	formula	perpendicular
diameter	circumference	isosceles	pentagonal
manipulative	trinomial	kilometer	exponential

Closing

- **What did we do today?** (*reviewed the process of analyzing long, unfamiliar words; read words from the subjects of science, social studies, and math*)
- **Why is it helpful to practice attacking long words?** (*builds up speed using the sequential strategy; assists in reading unfamiliar words; helps in spelling; promotes confidence for reading content area texts*)

Follow-Up

- Have each student find at least five new long words in a newspaper or textbook.
- Give students the opportunity to write one word on the board, and have other students try to analyze the word following the sequential process.
- Have students complete the activities in Handout 5.3.

Handout

5.3 Decoding Long Words (Practice 2)

Reminder

By now you know that in order to read long, unfamiliar words, it is useful to identify the language origin and then look for the morpheme units or break the word into syllables. If syllable division doesn't work, or works for only part of the word, you use letter-sound correspondences.

Activities

1. First, identify the origin of each word listed below and write it on the first line. Second, look for morphemes or break the words into syllables; count the number of syllables in each word and write it on the second line. Then, read each word.

Word	Origin	Syllables	Word	Origin	Syllables	Word	Origin	Syllables
monologue	Gk	3	autocracy	Gk	4	heliophobic	Gk	5
hyperkinetic	Gk	5	psychopathology	Gk	6	circumflexion	L	4
impossibility	L	6	incomprehensible	L	6	constellation	L	4
helioscope	Gk	4	hypothermal	Gk	4	weightlessness	A-S	3

2. Using some of the words above, complete each sentence below:

a. Children with ADHD are often __hyperkinetic__.

b. The terms __heliophobic__ and __helioscope__ both relate to the sun.

c. The astronaut achieved __weightlessness__ while in space.

d. __Psychopathology__ is a mental condition caused by disease.

e. My favorite __constellation__ is Orion.

Lesson

5.4 Spelling Long Words (Practice 1)

Opening

During the previous three lessons, we have read a number of words using a four-step strategy for analyzing those words. We can use a similar process as we spell long, new words.

Objective

Students will learn and use an analytical process to spell words.

Procedure

Today we'll spend most of the period spelling words. You won't have written some of these words before. Don't worry, just use this three-step process:

1. **Repeat the word that I dictate, and listen for common morphemes (affixes, roots, combining forms).**
2. **Listen for syllables and count them aloud or silently, as you say the syllables and write the words.**
3. **Use letter-sound correspondences when necessary.**

As you dictate the following words for students to **spell**, be sure students repeat each word; tell you the affixes, roots, or constituent words; break words into syllables if they can't find morphemes; and finally, use letter-sound correspondence. Students should always check their spelling after they write the word.

Feel free to substitute some of the words from the previous lessons or to use long, unfamiliar words from the student texts and readers. If you desire, put the words in sentences for students to **spell**. Get students in the habit of watching you as you say the word, listening carefully as you say the word alone, in a sentence, and then alone again. Students then follow the analytical process above.

NOTE: Students may find it useful to say the base word from a long word (e.g., *competition, "compete"; definition, "define"*).

unselfishly	humorous	dentistry
excellent	trustworthy	apprehensive
tormented	centennial	imprisoned
vindictive	unqualified	bewildered
corruptible	discouraged	antiseptic
thermometer	accumulate	convenient

Have students check their spelling as you write the words on the board.

Closing

- **What did we do today?** (*spelled multisyllabic words using a three-step process*)
- **Why is it helpful to practice spelling long words, even if we haven't studied and memorized them?** (*we can use these strategies with all words; it should expand our ability to spell as we practice breaking words into their parts*)

Follow-Up

- Dictate a number of related long words and see if students can write a paragraph based on these words.
- Have students complete the activities in Handout 5.4.

Handout

5.4 Spelling Long Words (Practice 1)

Reminder

Now we switch to strategies useful in spelling long, unfamiliar words. Use the following steps in spelling unknown words:

1. Repeat the word aloud and listen for common morphemes (affixes, roots, combining forms).
2. Listen for syllables and count them aloud or silently as you say the syllables and write the words.
3. Use letter-sound correspondences when necessary.

Activities

1. Here are 12 words using Latin word roots:

incredulous	spectacular	manuscript
misinformed	manufacturer	attractive
vindictive	nonreflective	curriculum
perceptible	subaudible	instrumentalists

Write the words in alphabetical order:

attractive
curriculum
incredulous
instrumentalists
manufacturer
manuscript
misinformed
nonreflective
perceptible
spectacular
subaudible
vindictive

2. Use some of the words above to complete these sentences:

The fireworks were ___spectacular___. We were all ___incredulous___ of the amazing display. Some spectators missed the show as they were ___misinformed___ about the time. The ___instrumentalists___ in the band accompanied the fireworks.

3. Use at least 2 words from the list above in each sentence that you compose below:

a. ______________________________

b. ______________________________

c. ______________________________

Lesson

5.5 Spelling Long Words (Practice 2)

Opening

During the last lesson, we learned a sequential strategy for spelling long, unfamiliar words. We'll continue spelling more words using that strategy today.

Objective

Students will review the strategy for spelling polysyllabic words and spell more words.

Procedure

Who remembers what we should do after we listen carefully to the dictated word? (*(1) repeat the word and listen for common morphemes (affixes, roots, combining forms); (2) listen for syllables and count them aloud or silently; (3) use letter-sound correspondences when necessary*)

Today we'll spend most of our time spelling more words. Many of these will be new to you, but if you use the three-step process we discussed, you will be successful.

Use the steps described in Lesson 5.4 as you dictate the following words (or other long words of your choice) for students to **spell**:

geography	phenomenon	approximate
unscrupulous	nondescript	overwhelming
veterinarian	irregular	flexibility
monorail	syllable	representative
bibliography	physiology	metropolis

Closing

What did we do today? (spelled multisyllabic words using a three-step process)

Who remembers why it is helpful to practice spelling long words, even if we haven't studied and memorized them? (we can use these strategies with all words; it can expand the ability to spell as we practice breaking words into their parts)

Let students know that in the next two lessons, they will review important spelling rules and patterns taught in earlier units.

Follow-Up

- Encourage students to keep a list of unfamiliar long words in their notebooks. If you have 10–15 minutes of extra time, ask students to write sentences or a paragraph using some of these words.
- Have students complete the activities in Handout 5.5.

Handout

5.5 Spelling Long Words (Practice 2)

Reminder

We use the following steps in spelling unknown words:

1. Repeat the word aloud and listen for common morphemes (affixes, roots, combining forms).
2. Listen for syllables and count them aloud or silently as you say the syllables and write the words.
3. Use letter-sound correspondences when necessary.

Activities

1. Here are 12 words using Greek combining forms:

autobiography	dermatherapy	hydrodynamics
ecogeography	mediocracy	encyclopedia
synchronicity	heliosphere	hyperglycemia
philanthropist	telephotography	anthropomorphic

List the words in alphabetical order:

anthropomorphic
autobiography
dermatherapy
ecogeography
encyclopedia
heliosphere
hydrodynamics
hyperglycemia
mediocracy
philanthropist
synchronicity
telephotography

2. Use some of the words above to complete these sentences:

a. The ___philanthropist___ donated money to many deserving charities.

b. His diabetes caused ___hyperglycemia___.

c. We looked up treatment for skin diseases under ___dermatherapy___ in the ___encyclopedia___.

d. Frank Lloyd Wright's ___autobiography___ is filled with fascinating facts.

3. Use at least 2 words from the list above in each sentence that you compose below:

a. ______________________________

b. ______________________________

c. ______________________________

Spelling Rules for One-Syllable Words

Opening

During the previous lessons, we often spelled a number of words as we learned about different patterns and strategies helpful for reading and spelling. Today we will review spelling patterns typical in many one-syllable words.

NOTE: See the Spelling Rules section of this manual for a complete list of spelling patterns and rules.

Objective

Students will review spelling rules for common letter-sound correspondences in one-syllable words. Students will generate, read, and spell words containing these patterns.

Procedure

ff, ll, ss, zz

The letters *f, l, s,* and *z* are usually found doubled at the end of a one-syllable word immediately following a short vowel. Write the following words on the board. **Read the following words and notice that each *f, l, s,* and *z* follows a short vowel.**

ff

cuff buff doff cliff stiff skiff scoff
bluff fluff skiff

ll

kill skill shrill drill smell doll dull
mill still grill thrill bill sell skull
hill will bell well

ss

mass bass class mess dress miss muss

zz

jazz buzz fuzz fizz frizz

Common exceptions to this rule include *if, clef, gas, this, us, thus, yes, bus, plus,* and *quiz.*

Ask students to **spell** some of the words above or others fitting this rule.

ck, tch, dge

Write the patterns *ck, tch,* and *dge* as headings on the board. List examples below as you get students to discuss the similarities in the lists. See if students can **generate** the rule by looking at the examples.

1. We use *ck* to spell the /k/ sound if it comes immediately after one short vowel at the end of a one-syllable word.

stick	back	luck	deck	truck	clock	track
brick	peck	stuck	lick	sick	lack	crack
trick	pluck	stack	block	struck	speck	quack

2. We use *tch* to spell the /ch/ sound if it comes immediately after one short vowel at the end of a one-syllable word.

match	hutch	hitch	fetch	notch	crutch	stitch
patch	batch	Dutch	witch	scratch	latch	ditch

NOTE: There are four common exceptions to this rule: *much, such, which,* and *rich.*

3. We use *dge* to spell the /j/ sound if it comes immediately after one short vowel at the end of a one-syllable word. Note that without *dge*, the vowel would be long.

badge	fudge	judge	ledge	bridge	trudge	edge
wedge	nudge	ridge	hedge	grudge	sludge	pledge

(Depending on your students' ability, you may want to do one of these patterns per day. Include spelling dictation. Once the new patterns are learned, add mixed lists of words so that students can make decisions on whether to use final *k* or *ck*, *ch* or *tch*, and *ge* or *dge*. Remember that if the word has a long vowel sound (usually with a vowel digraph), or a consonant preceding the final consonant sound, the special spelling need not be used. For example, *beak, milk, brick; pouch, porch, hutch;* and *cage, large, badge.*)

Closing

- **What spelling patterns did we review today?** (*the use of* ff, ll, ss, zz *and* ck, tch, *and* dge)
- **Why are they useful?** (*these patterns are used in special situations and we need to know them to spell words correctly*)

Follow-Up

- Dictate two or three phrases or sentences that include words with the patterns taught.
- Have students complete the activities in Handout 5.6.

Handout

5.6 Spelling Rules for One-Syllable Words

In this lesson, we learned about rules affecting one-syllable words ending in *f*, *l*, *s*, and *z*, and also about the spelling of words ending in the sounds /k/, /ch/, and /j/. You will recall that *l*, *f*, *s*, and *z* are usually found doubled at the end of a one-syllable word immediately following a short vowel. In addition, we use *ck* to spell the /k/ sound if it comes immediately after one short vowel at the end of a one-syllable word, we use *tch* to spell the /ch/ sound if it comes immediately after one short vowel at the end of a one-syllable word, and we use *dge* to spell the /j/ sound if it comes immediately after one short vowel at the end of a one-syllable word.

NOTE: If you studied these four situations separately, do each activity on the days you studied each pattern.

Activities

1. Add *l*, *f*, *s*, and *z* or add final e to each word as required. When necessary, the macron (¯) and breve (˘) will mark the long and short vowel sounds, respectively.

jăz	sāf	grăs	drĕs
jazz	safe	grass	dress
grāz	flŭf	bŭz	greas
graze	fluff	buzz	grease
strīf	dŏl	hĭl	fĭl
strife	doll	hill	fill
mōl	stĭl	clăs	smīl
mole	still	class	smile

2. Why do the following words take *ck*?

rack	truck	click	deck
stick	crack	fleck	clock

The /k/ sound is at the end of a one-syllable word immediately following one short vowel.

3. Why don't the following words take *ck*?

milk	beak	hulk	shook
balk	peek	skunk	soak

They have a consonant or two vowels preceding the final /k/ sound.

4. Why do the following words take *tch*?

pitch	Dutch	clutch	match
notch	stitch	scratch	fetch

The /ch/ sound is at the end of a one-syllable word immediately following one short vowel.

5. Why don't the following words take *tch*?

pinch	peach	poach	couch
lunch	leech	mulch	ranch

They have a consonant or two vowels preceding the final /ch/ sound.

6. Why do the following words take *dge*?

grudge	bridge	badge	pledge
dodge	dredge	fudge	judge

The /j/ sound is at the end of a one-syllable word immediately following one short vowel.

7. Why don't the following words take *dge*?

lunge	cage	range	large
change	bilge	stage	plunge

They have a consonant or long vowel sound preceding the final /j/ sound.

8. Use words in the lists above to complete each sentence below:

a. Try to __dodge__ when you spill the __milk__ .

b. We enjoyed life on the range *or* ranch, especially when the __grass__ was green.

c. __Clutch__ the purse very tightly when you go to __fetch__ the mail.

d. The __truck__ went over the __bridge__ and tried not to __plunge__ into the water.

Spelling Rules for Adding Suffixes (Final *e*)

Opening

Today we will continue our work with frequently used spelling rules. In the next four lessons, we will review what to do when adding suffixes.

Objective

Students will review the spelling rule for adding suffixes to base words ending in consonant-*e*.

Procedure

There are three spelling rules that apply to adding suffixes to base (or root) words. Today we will review the silent-*e* rule.

As you present these base words, give students ample opportunity to spell the suffixed words from dictation.

When adding suffixes beginning with a vowel to words ending in a silent *e*, the *e* is dropped. (The long vowel sound is retained.)

care	cared	caring	But: careless, careful
like	liked	likable	But: likely
safe	safer	safest	But: safety
time	timed	timing	But: timely
care	cared	caring	But: careless
blame	blaming	blamed	But: blameless

In order to retain the soft sound of *c* and *g*, keep the silent *e* when adding the suffixes *-able* and *-ous*. Write the following words on the board. Read these words and discuss what would happen without the *e* on the end of the base word.

noticeable	enforceable	courageous	manageable
traceable	serviceable	changeable	chargeable

Also, the final *e* is kept in some cases to save the identity of the word. Write the following words on the board. Discuss what happens if the *e* on the end of the base word is dropped.

singeing	hoeing	shoeing	acreage
tingeing	dyeing	canoeing	mileage

Closing

- **Which rule for adding suffixes did we study today?** (*dropping final* e)
- **Who can restate that rule?** (*we usually drop the final* e *in the base word when the suffix begins with a vowel, unless dropping the* e *will change the pronunciation of the base word*)

Follow-Up

- Have students complete the activities in Handout 5.7.

Handout

5.7 Spelling Rules for Adding Suffixes (Final *e*)

Reminders

We usually drop the final, silent *e* when adding suffixes beginning with a vowel.

Sometimes we need to keep the silent *e* if dropping it will change the sound of a *c* or *g* (before suffixes beginning with *a* and *o*).

Activities

1. Use the silent-*e* rule to add the given suffix to the base word.

elope + ing = eloping

unlike + able = unlikable

revolve + er = revolver

misfire + ing = misfiring

blame + ing = blaming

blame + less = blameless

enforce + ing = enforcing

enforce + able = enforceable

singe + ing = singeing

hope + ful = hopeful

2. Using base words from above, add logical suffixes to make complete sentences below:

a. The couple eloped and went on their honeymoon.

b. They were very hopeful and hoped that the romance would last.

c. The earth revolves around the sun.

d. The judge tried enforcing the verdict.

e. He singed his eyebrows while grilling the steak.

3. Add suffixes to the following base words and write a sentence using each word:

time	place	devote	bake
use	care	share	like

a. ____________________

b. ____________________

c. ____________________

d. ______________________________

e. ______________________________

f. ______________________________

g. ______________________________

h. ______________________________

Lesson

5.8 Spelling Rules for Adding Suffixes (Doubling Rule)

Opening

Today we will continue our work with frequently used spelling rules.

Objective

Students will review the spelling rule for adding suffixes to base words ending in a single consonant, preceded by a vowel.

Procedure

Today we will review the doubling rule for both one-syllable and polysyllabic base words.

As you present these base words, give students ample opportunity to **spell** the suffixed words from dictation.

One-Syllable Base Words

When a base word ends with a single consonant, preceded by a vowel, double the final consonant if the suffix begins with a vowel.

sad	sadder	saddest
strap	strapped	strapping
fit	fitter	fittest
drop	dropper	dropping
cut	cutting	cutter

This rule relates to the vowel markers we discussed in Unit 1. If there were just one consonant, the preceding vowel would be long (e.g., *hopping* vs. *hoping*).

Words ending in two consonants, or having a vowel digraph, do not double a final consonant, because the vowel sound is already established.

dust	dusty
chant	chanting
last	lasted
cool	cooler
boil	boiling
deep	deepest

Also, you needn't double the final consonant if the suffix begins with a consonant.

hot	hotly
ship	shipment
fret	fretful
slim	slimness
drip	dripless
glad	gladly

Polysyllabic Base Words

NOTE: This is probably the most difficult rule for students with learning disabilities to internalize. Do not include it for younger students with reading problems. You may want to present this as a separate lesson for older students.

The doubling rule also applies to words of two or more syllables, provided the accent falls on the last syllable of the base word and the conditions discussed earlier are met.

begin'	beginning	beginner
admit'	admitted	admittance
forbid'	forbidden	forbidding
transmit'	transmitted	transmitting
excel'	excelled	excellent
permit'	permitted	permitting

NOTE: If you have students that can't hear accent, don't dwell on this problem. Let students know that most Latin roots get the accent and thus will double the consonant, but only if there is a single consonant. On the other hand, words with no common root (often of Anglo-Saxon origin) will not have the accent on the last syllable. For example, *mar'/ket, marketed; gar'/den, gardening; o'/pen, opening.* Of note is the fact that newer dictionaries are providing two alternative spellings for many words without the accent on the last syllable (e.g., *traveling, travelling; marketed, marketted*).

As mentioned in an earlier unit, there are exceptions to this rule, especially for the roots *fit* and *fir. Offer, suffer,* and *differ* never double the final *r,* no matter what suffix is added. Other *fer* words do double, but only with the suffixes *-ed, -ing,* and *-al.*

Fit* is even more complex. Anglo-Saxon words having to do with size or clothing do double: *misfit, misfitting; befit, befitting; outfit, outfitted.* Yet Latin-based words do not double: *profit, profitable; discomfit, discomfiting; benefit, benefited.

Closing

What did we study today? (*the doubling rule for adding suffixes*)

Who can summarize the rules for doubling final consonants? (*when a base word ends with a single consonant preceded by a vowel, double the final consonant if the suffix begins with a vowel; in words of two or more syllables, double the final consonant only if the accent falls on the last syllable of the base word*)

Follow-Up

- Have students complete the activities in Handout 5.8.

Handout

5.8 Spelling Rules for Adding Suffixes (Doubling Rule)

Reminders

This lesson reminded you that when a one-syllable base word ends with a single consonant, preceded by a vowel, you double the final consonant if the suffix begins with a vowel.

The doubling rule also applies to words of two or more syllables, provided the accent falls on the last syllable of the base word, the word ends with a single consonant preceded by a vowel, and the suffix begins with a vowel.

Refer to Lesson 5.8 for information about adding suffixes to the roots *fer* and *fit.*

Activities

1. Add the suffix to each base word. Double the final consonant when necessary.

grab + ed = grabbed
sketch + ing = sketching
drop + ing = dropping
sad + est = saddest
hit + less = hitless
care + ful = careful
shrug + ed = shrugged
green + er = greener

2. Now add the suffix to each multisyllabic base word. Double the final consonant when necessary. (It may help to mark the accent on the base word.)

begin + ing = beginning
permit + ed = permitted
excel + ent = excellent
market + ed = marketed
open + ing = opening
forgot + en = forgotten
transform + ing = transforming
transmit + ing = transmitting

3. Add suffixes to the following words to complete each sentence logically.

permit	slim	forbid	grab
swim	travel	mud	big

a. The swimmer was permitted to dive into the pool.

b. She was slimmer than ever after traveling in Africa.

c. He was forbidden to enter the muddy graveyard at night.

d. We grabbed the biggest donkey by the tail.

Spelling Rules for Adding Suffixes (Final *y*)

Opening

Today we will continue our work with frequently used spelling rules.

Objective

Students will review the spelling rule for adding suffixes to base words ending in the letter *y*.

Procedure

Today we will review adding suffixes to words ending in the letter *y*. As you present these words, give students ample opportunity to **spell** words from dictation.

Words ending in *y* preceded by a vowel just add the suffix.

play	played	player
buy	buyer	buying
enjoy	enjoyable	enjoyment
stray	straying	strayed

Words ending in *y* preceded by a consonant change the *y* to *i* when adding a suffix, unless the suffix begins with the letter *i*.

empty	emptied	But: emptying
silly	sillier	silliest
easy	easily	easier
spy	spied	But: spying
copy	copier	But: copyist
early	earliest	earlier
apply	appliance	But: applying
victory	victorious	
fry	fried	But: frying
fly	flier	But: flying

Closing

- What did we study today? (*reviewed the final-y rule for adding suffixes*)
- Who can summarize the rule for adding suffixes to words ending in y? (*words ending in* y *preceded by a consonant change the* y *to* i *when adding a suffix, unless the suffix begins with the letter* i)

Follow-Up

- Provide practice by dictating phrases and/or sentences with words using these rules.
- Have students complete the activities in Handout 5.9.

Handout

5.9 Spelling Rules for Adding Suffixes (Final *y*)

Reminder

Remember that we often change the final *y* in a base word to add a suffix. This happens unless a vowel precedes the final *y* (as in *stay*), or the suffix begins with the letter *i* (as in *trying*).

Activities

1. Add the suffix to each base word. Change the *y* to *i* if necessary.

play + ed = played	empty + ed = emptied
enjoy + ment = enjoyment	empty + ing = emptying
apply + ance = appliance	apply + ing = applying
fly + er = flier	fly + ing = flying

2. Add the suffix to each base word. Change the *y* to *i* if necessary. Then use the words to complete each sentence below.

copy + ist = copyist	copy + ed = copied
glory + ous= glorious	story + es = stories
victory + ous = victorious	spy + ing = spying

a. He told glorious stories of the past.

b. The copyist copied the manuscript.

c. The victorious soldier had been spying on the enemy.

3. Divide each word into its base and suffix.

a. helpful = help + ful

b. funniest = funny + est

c. strayed = stray + ed

d. babies = baby + es

e. carrying = carry + ing

f. silliest = silly + est

Lesson

5.10 Practice for Rule-Based Words

Opening

Today we will have a chance to spell phrases and sentences using the rules we have just reviewed.

Objective

Students will spell phrases and sentences using the rules they have recently reviewed.

Procedure

Today I'm going to dictate several phrases and sentences for you to *spell*. The phrases will include words that use the rules we have studied in our last few lessons.

See if students can apply their spelling rules to the following phrases and sentences. Be sure students repeat each word and say the base word of any affixed words before **spelling**.

Phrases

slammed the pitch	lifeless performance
widest bridge	a movable wedge
snobbish witch	expensive crutch
cooked the fudge	outrageous clock
scanned the badge	biggest excitement
timely action	racing to the dock

Dictate the following sentences to students for them to **spell**:

- The babies all cried loudly.
- He had an enjoyable dinner in the dining room.
- He copied the information on the serviceable machine.

Closing

- **What did we do today?** (*spelled phrases and sentences containing rule-based words*)
- **Why does it help to understand some of the spelling rules?** (*helps you to spell words correctly*)
- **How can this help you as you are writing book reports, research papers, and stories?** (*helps you spell words correctly*)

Follow-Up

- As you have free time, dictate several phrases or sentences to review students' understanding of rules, morphemes, syllables, and other concepts. This way, you'll know what you need to review when you have time in the future.
- Remind the students to use the strategies they have worked on as they get new reading and writing assignments.
- Have students complete the activities in Handout 5.10.

Handout 5.10 Practice for Rule-Based Words

Reminder

This handout gives you practice using some of the rules you have just studied and reviewed. You can go back to other handouts to review if you wish.

Activities

1. Write sentences using the following phrases:

   a. hopeful attitude: ______

   b. snobbish actress: ______

   c. outrageous habits: ______

   d. profitable business: ______

   e. youngest conductor: ______

2. What is the language origin of all of the following words?

flying	blackboard	babyish	kingdom
pilot	trickster	muddiest	skating

   a. Anglo-Saxon

   b. How do you know? Short, common everyday words; some compounds, some with affixes.

3. What is the language origin of all of the following words?

conductor	inspection	inactive	manufacture
predicted	controversy	extracting	abruptly

   a. Latin

   b. How do you know? Each contains a root and affixes; polysyllabic.

4. What is the language origin of all of the following words?

phonograph	thermometer	telegram	autobiography
dermatology	dialogue	octagon	tricycle

a. Greek

b. How do you know? They are scientific words, contain combining forms, and have some unique Greek letter-sound correspondences.

Lesson 5.11 Review of Strategies for Decoding and Spelling Long, Unfamiliar Words

Opening

Today we will review the strategies for analyzing words that are new, long, and/or unfamiliar to you. This will be the end of our units on word study.

Objective

Students will review the sequence for reading new words and then read and spell polysyllabic words.

Procedure

Who remembers the four-step sequence for reading new words? ((1) identify word origin if possible; (2) look for morphemes; (3) break the word into syllables; (4) use letter-sound correspondence)

Who remembers the three-step sequence for spelling new words? ((1) listen carefully for morphemes; (2) listen for syllables and count them aloud or silently; (3) use letter-sound correspondences when necessary)

Ask students to **read** the following words after you write them on the board:

accumulation	evaporation	artichoke
indoctrinate	contaminate	conspicuous
responsibility	colonialism	chlorophyll
ammunition	compromise	combustible

Ask students to **spell** the following words:

elastic	diplomat	independent
absolutely	establishment	electrocute
photograph	phonogram	unicycle

Closing

- Review how having strategies for reading and spelling unfamiliar words results in reading and spelling more accurately.

Follow-Up

- Have students complete the activities in Handout 5.11.
- Administer the Unit 5 Quiz found on the CD.
- Although this unit concludes the *Words* program, continue to evaluate all students' reading and spelling problems so that you can review and supplement the activities.

Handout

5.11 Review of Strategies for Decoding and Spelling Long, Unfamiliar Words

Reminders

You now have learned several strategies for reading and spelling unknown words.

In reading, you can look for morpheme patterns like prefixes, suffixes, base words, and roots; you can divide words into syllables; and you can figure out letters and their corresponding sounds.

In spelling, you know to repeat the word, listening for morphemes, saying it slowly in syllables and using the sounds you hear. You can use these sounds and syllables to write the word.

Activities

1. Read the following words. Use your new strategies to figure them out.

engagement	miniaturize	desolation	resuscitate
transactional	wizardry	deterioration	retrospective
pneumonia	antemeridian	nonagenarian	demisemiquaver

2. Choose a word from above to match each definition. You can use your dictionary.

   a. In music, a 32nd note: demisemiquaver

   b. Taking place in the morning: antemeridian

   c. A person in her 90s: nonagenarian

   d. To make on a greatly reduced scale: miniaturize

   e. To restore consciousness: resuscitate

   f. The art or skill of witchcraft: wizardry

3. Write logical sentences using the other six words:

   a. ______________________________

   ____

   b. ______________________________

   ____

Student Handout Answers

c. ______________________________

____

d. ______________________________

____

e. ______________________________

____

f. ______________________________

____

Unit Quizzes

Directions for Teachers:

1. Tell students they will take a brief quiz to review the topics you have been discussing in the unit. Tell them to try their best. If they can't complete a section, they should go on to the next section when you read those instructions.
2. Have students fill in their names, grade, and teacher at the top of the page.
3. Read the instructions for each quiz item aloud to your students as they read along. Do not define the underlined words, and do not read any of the word choices to the students.
4. Try not to expose the students to the spelling words used in these quizzes (see below) during your instruction.
5. Below are the spelling words to be dictated for each unit. Ask students to listen carefully and then to repeat the word before spelling it. Encourage students to sound out the words by letter-sound or syllable. (Before *h* in Units 1 through 5, notify students that the last word is not a real word; it is a nonsense word.)

Unit 1	Unit 2	Unit 3	Unit 4	Unit 5
a. pouch	a. banner	a. flashlight	a. compartment	a. acrobat
b. crawl	b. sampan	b. airplane	b. discharged	b. establishment
c. moist	c. nutmeg	c. overcome	c. imported	c. metronome
d. whale	d. sedan	d. thankful	d. inventor	d. heliograph
e. blast	e. crisis	e. helplessness	e. assertive	e. rejuvenate
f. diner	f. tribute	f. translate	f. biography	f. incredulous
g. grinned	g. create	g. telegram	g. physician	g. hibernate

Nonsense words (except for Unit 5):

h. brumming	h. lepformin	h. superdiction	h. hypergraphic	h. predicament
				i. intelligent
				j. tempestuous
				k. hectogram
				l. promptitude

6. Use the test results to determine the patterns and concepts that need additional instruction.

Unit 1 Quiz

Name: ____________ Grade: ________ Teacher: ____________

1. Circle any short vowels you find in the following words:

cat	pick	thump	vote	point
best	made	thrust	vault	strip

2. Circle any blends you find in the following words (some may have more than one):

thump	blast	scrap	pick	stand
vote	point	string	ouch	gruff
grade	produce	haunt	briefly	indoors

3. Circle any consonant digraphs you find in the following words (some may have more than one):

thump	blast	thing	point	thrush
when	porch	spot	ideal	nuthatch
church	thunder	shutter	whereby	thick

4. Circle any vowel digraphs you find in the following words:

vote	moist	shout	recall	floating
pick	thunder	flaunt	grief	achieve
enjoy	display	rescue	fawn	disappoint

5. Spell the words as your teacher dictates them to you:

a. pouch b. crawl

c. moist d. whale

e. blast f. diner

g. grinned h. brumming

Unit 2 Quiz

Name: ________________ Grade: ________ Teacher: ________________

1. Divide these words into syllables:

muf|fin ten|nis rab|bit mit|ten cab|bage
car|pet cat|nip cam|pus pet|rol cut|let

2. Divide these words into syllables:

ri|val pi|lot cab|in ro|dent de|mon
cam|el ban|ish hab|it mu|sic re|fine

3. Divide these words into syllables:

can|dle sad|dle bot|tle ta|ble thim|ble
pur|ple bu|gle ri|fle puz|zle wres|tle

4. Divide these words into syllables:

cre|ate o|a|sis vi|o|lin ar|cha|ic the|a|tre
va|ca|tion ar|ti|choke in|fec|ted pre|am|ble co|op|er|ate

5. Spell the words as your teacher dictates them to you.

a. banner b. sampan

c. nutmeg d. sedan

e. crisis f. tribute

g. create h. lepformin

Unit 3 Quiz

Name: ____________ Grade: ________ Teacher: ____________

1. Circle any words you find from the Anglo-Saxon layer of language:

(cow)	(mother)	(friend)	constructed	(love)
(cry)	(cough)	(where)	(flashlight)	television
(want)	(green)	reject	(railroad)	architect

2. Circle any words you find from the Latin (Romance) layer of language:

(subtracted)	bigger	(spectator)	autograph
(reflected)	(important)	rabbit	(corrupted)
(conducive)	(dejection)	eat	phonograph

3. Circle any words you find from the Greek layer of language:

(microscope)	(phonograph)	lovely	(hydrogen)
eruption	expedition	(biography)	sister
(hemisphere)	extracted	(telegraph)	(hyperthermal)

4. Spell the words as your teacher dictates them to you:

a. flashlight b. airplane

c. overcome d. thankful

e. helplessness f. translate

g. telegram h. superdiction

Unit 4 Quiz

Name: ____________ Grade: ________ Teacher: ____________

1. Circle any prefixes you find in the following words:

misread	distrust	subject	transfer
convene	along	became	unhappy
corrupt	illegal	safety	production

2. Circle any suffixes you find in the following words:

tremendous	reality	running	produced
population	captive	compound	final
realize	elevator	elevate	verify

3. Circle any Latin word roots you find in the following words:

information	returned	extracted	coldest
inspector	dictator	reflection	misspelled
campus	intensely	audience	suffered

4. Spell the words as your teacher dictates them to you:

a. compartment
b. discharged
c. imported
d. inventor
e. assertive
f. biography
g. physician
h. hypergraphic

Unit 5 Quiz

Name: ______________ Grade: ________ Teacher: ______________

1. How many syllables are in the following words? Read the words and write the number of syllables in the blank next to the word.

   a. vacation 3
   b. surprise 2
   c. artichoke 3
   d. proletariat 5
   e. argumentative 5
   f. fallacious 3
   g. cutaneous 4
   h. electromagnetic 6
   i. parsimonious 5
   j. symphonic 3

2. Spell the words as your teacher dictates them to you:

   a. acrobat
   b. establishment
   c. metronome
   d. heliograph
   e. rejuvenate
   f. incredulous
   g. hibernate
   h. predicament
   i. intelligent
   j. tempestuous
   k. hectogram
   l. promptitude

Posttest

Directions for Teachers:

Ask students to fill in their first and last names, grade, and the date on the top of the Posttest.

Numbers 1–12: Word Structure

Tell students you will ask them to circle parts of the words listed in the first few sections of the test. Let them know that some words may not contain the target word part. (During the test, remind students not to circle the whole word, only the part requested.)

Have students find number 1 on the Posttest. Read aloud the first line following number 1 on the test as the students read along silently.

NOTE: Do not define the underlined words, although you may repeat the key phrase (e.g., the *consonants*). Also, do not read any of the words to the students. In many cases, they won't have to read the words to identify the word parts.

Give students 60–90 seconds to complete the section. Then point out number 2, read the directions, and give 60–90 seconds to complete number 2. Continue in this manner through number 12.

1. Circle the <u>consonants</u> in the following words:

cub	pan	fix	robe
vacuum	jewel	baby	Pacific
journalist	energetic	exemption	frantically

2. Circle the <u>vowels</u> in the following words:

rob	have	zoom	thick
robot	motel	filthy	disappoint
instructor	evolve	undesirable	transportation

3. Circle any <u>short vowels</u> you find in the following words:

lip	cute	black	pinch
text	dumpling	bliss	mobster
misplace	distend	intact	symphony

4. Circle any <u>long vowels</u> you find in the following words:

cute	glide	slime	slimmer

prescribe	remote	virus	utilize
relocate	emotion	triumphant	hypothetical

5. Circle the blends in the following words:

blast	grove	plump	globe
twig	brush	trumpet	restrictive
silk	script	flourish	playful

6. Circle any consonant digraphs you find in the following words:

theme	chirp	whirl	thrash
chilly	bathe	moment	shutter
whitish	shimmer	grouchy	therapy

7. Circle any vowel digraphs you find in the following words:

haul	clue	proud	spool
pronoun	receiver	exploit	gloomy
hobo	reclaim	raincoat	retrieve

8. Divide the compound words into two word parts:

pancake	classroom	bathtub	giggle
flatboat	barefoot	hardship	milkman
iceberg	lamppost	toothpaste	motorboat

9. Circle any prefixes you find in the following words:

forgiven	indoor	unlikely	beholden
subways	disliking	mistaken	informal
alighting	expended	balloon	preventive

10. Circle the roots, or base words, in the following words:

inform	along	transport	convicted
twilight	misspell	auditorium	supervision
predictable	compulsive	convertible	subtracted

11. Circle any suffixes you find in the following words:

blinked	unhelpful	alone	conductor
reactive	transmission	generous	hungrily
magician	annoyance	beneficial	convertible

12. Draw a line between the syllables in these words:

copper	bargain	delightful	remit
collapse	coincide	commander	optimal
rejection	urbanization	nervously	cumulative

Number 13: Word Recognition

Dictate the following words to be circled from among the four words next to each letter. Give 15–20 seconds per item. (Before *q*, notify students that the next four words are not real words; they are nonsense words.)

a. really	b. crashed	c. export
d. hastily	e. beyond	f. kindly
g. business	h. congregate	i. quest
j. slimy	k. thistle	l. thorough
m. retire	n. secretive	o. impossible
p. espectfully		

Nonsense words:

q. frouch (/ou/ as in out)	r. sprĕg (rhymes with leg)	s. trănlĭnfĭx
t. brŏplăntĭc		

Number 14: Spelling

Dictate the following words to be spelled by the students. Tell students you will read the word once, give it in a sentence, and say the single word again. Students should be reminded to look at you while you say the word. Give students 20–25 seconds to write each word on their Posttest next to the appropriate letter. (Before *n*, notify students that the next three words are not real words; they are nonsense words.)

a. crawl	Crawl under the bed.	crawl
b. stool	Sit on the high stool.	stool
c. return	Return from the meeting soon.	return
d. unlikely	He was an unlikely candidate.	unlikely
e. displease	Try not to displease your mom.	displease
f. misspell	We won't misspell the words.	misspell
g. overhead	The balloons flew overhead.	overhead
h. visible	The crescent moon was visible.	visible
i. conductor	He was a famous conductor.	conductor
j. phonograph	Murray found the old phonograph.	phonograph
k. through	Walk through the woods.	through
l. among	My iPod is among my favorite gifts.	among
m. friendly	She was friendly toward the animals.	friendly

Nonsense words:

n. strōpe
o. crĭmtĕl
p. wĭlbăndŏk

Posttest

Name: ______________ Grade: ________ Teacher: ______________

1. Circle the consonants in the following words:

cub	pan	fix	robe
vacuum	jewel	baby	Pacific
journalist	energetic	exemption	frantically

2. Circle the vowels in the following words:

rob	have	zoom	thick
robot	motel	filthy	disappoint
instructor	evolve	undesirable	transportation

3. Circle any short vowels you find in the following words:

lip	cute	black	pinch
text	dumpling	bliss	mobster
misplace	distend	intact	symphony

4. Circle any long vowels you find in the following words:

cute	glide	slime	slimmer
prescribe	remote	virus	utilize
relocate	emotion	triumphant	hypothetical

5. Circle the blends in the following words:

blast	grove	plump	globe
twig	brush	trumpet	restrictive
silk	script	flourish	playful

6. Circle any consonant digraphs you find in the following words:

theme	chirp	whirl	thrash
chilly	bathe	moment	shutter
whitish	shimmer	grouchy	therapy

7. Circle any vowel digraphs you find in the following words:

haul	clue	proud	spool
pronoun	receiver	exploit	gloomy
hobo	reclaim	raincoat	retrieve

Student Handout Answers

8. Divide the compound words into two word parts:

pan|cake class|room bath|tub giggle
flat|boat bare|foot hard|ship milk|man
ice|berg lamp|post tooth|paste motor|boat

9. Circle any prefixes you find in the following words:

forgiven indoor unlikely beholden
subways disliking mistaken informal
alighting expended balloon preventive

10. Circle the roots, or base words, in the following words:

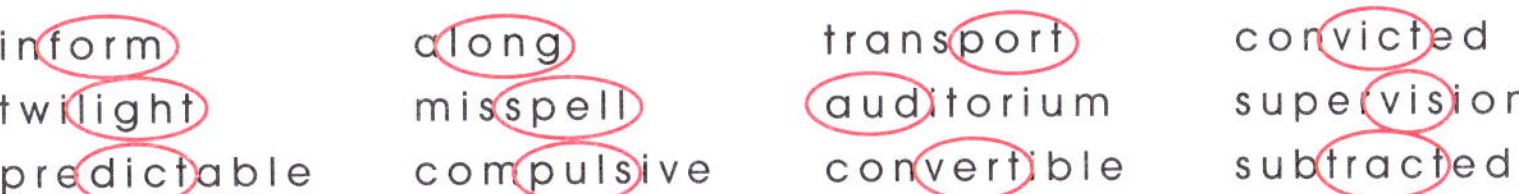

inform along transport convicted
twilight misspell auditorium supervision
predictable compulsive convertible subtracted

11. Circle any suffixes you find in the following words:

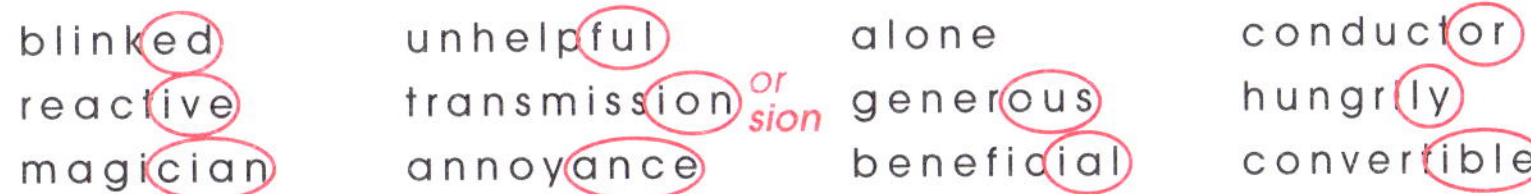

blinked unhelpful alone conductor
reactive transmission *or sion* generous hungrily
magician annoyance beneficial convertible

12. Draw a line between the syllables in these words:

cop|per bar|gain de|light|ful re|mit
col|lapse co|in|cide com|man|der op|ti|mal
re|jec|tion ur|ban|i|za|tion ner|vous|ly cu|mu|la|tive

or com/mand/er

13. For each group of four words, circle the word dictated by your teacher:

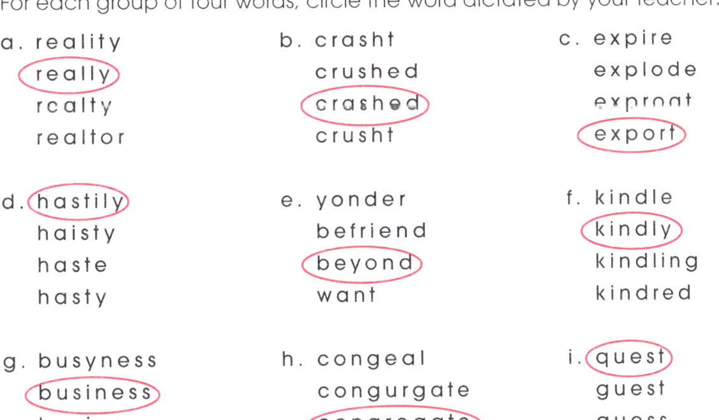

a. reality
really
rcalty
realtor

b. crasht
crushed
crashed
crusht

c. expire
explode
exproat
export

d. hastily
haisty
haste
hasty

e. yonder
befriend
beyond
want

f. kindle
kindly
kindling
kindred

g. busyness
business
busier
busied

h. congeal
congurgate
congregate
congress

i. quest
guest
guess
quiver

POSTTEST

96

Posttest

Student Handout Answers

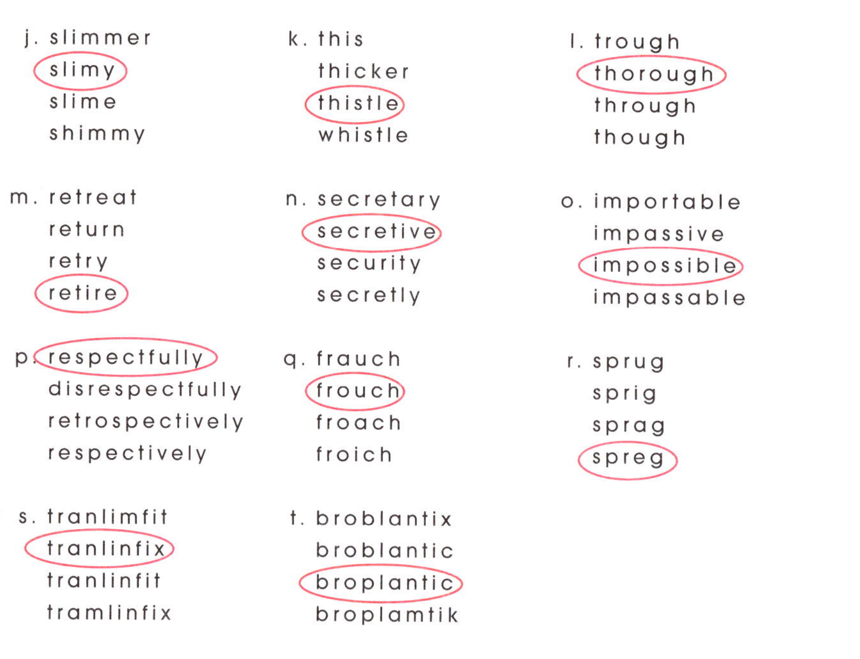

j. slimmer
slimy
slime
shimmy

k. this
thicker
thistle
whistle

l. trough
thorough
through
though

m. retreat
return
retry
retire

n. secretary
secretive
security
secretly

o. importable
impassive
impossible
impassable

p. **respectfully**
disrespectfully
retrospectively
respectively

q. frauch
frouch
froach
froich

r. sprug
sprig
sprag
spreg

s. tranlimfit
tranlinfix
tranlinfit
tramlinfix

t. broblantix
broblantic
broplantic
broplamtik

14. Spell the words as your teacher dictates them to you:

a. crawl
b. stool
c. return
d. unlikely
e. displease
f. misspell
g. overhead
h. visible
i. conductor
j. phonograph
k. through
l. among
m. friendly
n. strope *or* stroap
o. crimtel, crimtell, crymtel, *or* crymtell
p. wilbandok, willbandoc, wilbandok, *or* willbandok

Non-Phonetic Words

Directions for Teachers:

1. Show students the non-phonetic (irregular) word and tell what it says.
2. Write a model of the word for students to trace, copy, write, and say letter names, followed by the name of the word.
3. Be sure students understand why the non-phonetic word needs to be memorized (i.e., why it doesn't follow the phonetic principle). Point out that consonants usually follow direct letter-sound correspondence, while vowels do not.

The following words are among the most frequently used irregular words:

List 1

the	a	have	of	off
one	only	do	to	two
does	was	want	were	what
where	there	they	are	again
says	said	you	your	yours
who	any	many	been	other
some	come	from	through	very
put	push	pull	door	floor
their	often	would	could	should
friend	walk	talk	love	gone

List 2

give	live	whose	whom	whole
sure	month	son	won	buy
build	busy	among	nothing	front
move	against	listen	pretty	people
laugh	rough	tough	enough	cough
Wednesday	February	clothes	sew	iron
heart	eye	toward	though	thorough
half	pint	ninth	answer	soft
wind	such	much	rich	which
beautiful	prove	great	steak	break
straight	touch	ocean	island	lose
shoe	sugar	wore	worn	swore
hour	honest	honor	usual	flood
blood	truth	doubt	debt	height
calf	wolf	muscle	guess	guest
guy	guide	guard		

Assorted Word Lists

Words of Latin Origin

introduction
interruption
corruption
destructive
bilateral
professor
superstitious
extracted
exclusively
transformation
circumscribe
circumference
impulsive
dejected
intermission
dictatorship
unintentionally
diverted
averted
rupture

reception
literature
respectfully
predictable
cooperate
inaudible
incredulous
prescription
convention
contracted
information
detention
convertible
interjection
admittance
reflector
dependent
independent
interdependence
structure

difference
competence
adversity
reflection
observant
subtraction
spectacular
prescribing
corruptible
disrespectful
contradict
manufacture
extrovert
introvert
dictaphone
suspension
pendant
projection
attention
spectator

Words of Greek Origin

chronometer
physician
physiology
physiologist
telegraph
metropolis
metropolitan
hemisphere
decameter
pentathlon
biathlon
psychology
psychologist
hydroplane
dermatology
polygon
octagon

perimeter
zoology
biography
bibliography
autobiography
hyperactive
hypoactive
hydrogen
monorail
television
telegram
telemetry
monologue
dialogue
systematic
syllable
sympathy

microscope
periscope
telescope
architect
archeology
phonograph
photograph
autograph
triangle
autocrat
autocracy
semicircle
microcosm
symphonic
orthodontist
periodontist
pedometer

Words for Lesson 5.1

List 1

pretending
understandable
prevention
reduction
thunderhead
dangerous
boisterous
surrounding
exclusive
government
consideration
reconstructionist
autograph
disturbance
devotion
moisture
memorandum
gymnasium
incredible

List 2

incongruous
superstitious
accumulation
hippopotamus
illustrious
corruptible
flamboyant
boisterous
maladroit
moisture
cantankerous
semaphore
ophthalmoscope
ambulatory
acquaintance
extraordinary
pejorative
calumniously
euphemism

Science and Social Studies Words for Lesson 5.2

Science Words

spontaneous
microorganism
electromagnetism
abiogenesis
clarification
galvanometer
investigation
imaginary
experiment
frequency
infrared
ultraviolet
spectrum
photosynthesis

Social Studies Words

bicentennial
guaranteed
legislation
unrealistic
colonization
essentially
hierarchy
proletariat
argumentative
sequential
ideology
oppressor
communism
socialism

Content Area Words for Lesson 5.3

Science

assumption
ionization
molecular
activation
catalysts
reactants
subcutaneous
subserous
visceral
extensibility
tendonitis
archaeology
illumination
intelligence
neurosurgeon
nitrogenous
myofilaments
hemodialysis
vertebrates
erythrocytes
fibrinogen
epidermis
zoology
experimental
laboratory
hypotheses
behavioral
variable
theoretical
spectroheliograph
orthodontist
momentum
physics
chemistry

Social Studies

perpetuate
dictatorship
peasants
dogma
caricature
elaborately
judicial
executive
presidential
electoral
columnists
politicians

Math

mathematician
statistics
dividend
quadrangle
bilateral
calculus
polygon
probability
quotient
estimate
simultaneous
computation
binomial
symbols
formula
perpendicular
diameter
circumference
isosceles

Prefixes Expressing Number

Key: (L) = Latin; (G) = Greek

1 = *uni-* (L) uniform, unicorn, universe *mono-* (G) monograph, monogram

2 = *bi-* (L) bicycle, biceps, bifocal, biplane *di-* (G) digraph, dioxide

3 = *tri-* (L & G) triangle, triangular, tricycle, tripod

4 = *quar-, quadr-* (L) quart, quarter, quadrangle, quadruple
tetra- (G) tetrahedron, tetrameter

5 = *quint-* (L) quintet, quintuplet *pent-* (G) pentagon, pentathlon

6 = *sex-* (L) sextet, sextant, sextuple *hex-* (G) hexagon, hexagram

7 = *sept-* (L) September, septuagenarian *hept-* (G) heptagon, heptameter

8 = *octo-* (L & G) October, octet, octagon, octopus

9 = *nona-, nove-* (L) nonagenarian, nonagon, November, novena

10 = *dec-, deca-, deci-* (G) decade, decathalon, decigram, December, decimal, decimeter

100 = *cent-* (L) centigrade, century, cent, centigram, centimeter, centiliter
hect- (G) hectogram, hectometer, hectare

1,000 = *milli-* (L) milligram, millimeter, million, millisecond
kilo- (G) kilogram, kilometer, kilowatt, kiloliter

10,000 = *myria-* (G) myriameter, myriad

million = *mega-* (G) megameter (*mega-* also means *large size*)

billion = *giga-* (G) gigameter, gigahertz

trillion = *tera-* (G) terameter, terahertz

quadrillion = *peta-* (G) petameter

quintillion = *exa-* (G) exameter

Spelling Rules

The English spelling system has several rule-categories that hold firm for almost all words in each category. Apply these spelling rules before considering exceptions to the rules.

Silent *e*

a. Silent *e* on the end of a word "makes" the single vowel immediately preceding the final *e* long (i.e., makes it say its name; sometimes called the *magic e rule*).

b. Silent *e* makes y = /ī /, as in *type, style.*

c. Final *ve:* A preceding single vowel may or may not be long before ve.

Examples: ***five, gave, drove*** **(long vowel sound)**

Exceptions: ***have, give, love*** **(Students should memorize these.)**

ff, ll, ss, zz

Double a final *l, f, s,* and sometimes *z* immediately following a single vowel in one-syllable words.

Examples: ***tell, staff, grass, buzz***

Exceptions: ***if, clef, gas, this, us, thus, yes, bus, plus, quiz*** **(Students should memorize these.)**

NOTE: Final *s* as /z/ is never doubled (e.g., *as, is, was, has, his*).

Soft *c* and *g*

The letters *c* and *g* have a soft sound when they appear directly before *e, i,* and *y.*

a. *c* = /s/ before *e, i,* and *y.*

Examples: ***center, city, cycle***

b. *g* = /j/ before *e, i,* and *y.*

Examples: ***gentle, ginger, gym***

(1) Exceptions do not present spelling problems, because in such exceptions, the *g* has its hard sound.

Examples: ***get, give, buggy, bigger***

(2) The letter *g* is always used for the /j/ sound before the letter *y*.

Examples: ***gym, gypsy, apology***

ck, tch, dge

The patterns *ck, tch,* and *dge* are used to say /k/, /ch/, and /j/, respectively, when the sounds come at the end of a word, immediately after one short vowel.

a. ***ck:*** Use *ck* to spell the /k/ sound immediately after one short vowel at the end of a one-syllable word.

Examples: ***back, clock, duck***

b. ***tch:*** Use *tch* to spell the /ch/ sound after one short vowel at the end of a one-syllable word, and also in a few two-syllable words.

Examples: ***patch, itch, stretch, kitchen***

Exceptions: ***such, much, rich, which*** **(These should be memorized.)**

c. ***dge:*** Use *dge* to spell the /j/ sound immediately after one short vowel at the end of a one-syllable word.

Examples: ***judge, bridge, dodge***

Adding Suffixes

a. **Dropping final *e:*** When a base word ends with final e, drop the e before adding a suffix starting with a vowel.

Examples: ***blame - blaming*** **(But:** ***blameless*****);** ***take - taking; fine - finer*** **(But:** ***finely*****);** ***stone - stony***

b. **Double-letter rule**

(1) **One-syllable words:** In a one-syllable word, with one short vowel (a closed syllable), ending in one consonant, double the final consonant before a suffix starting with a vowel (*-ed, -er, -ing, -y,* etc.). Do not double the final consonant before a suffix starting with a consonant (*-ful, -ly, -ment, -ness,* etc.).

Examples: ***fit - fitted*** **(But:** ***fitful*****);** ***sad - sadder*** **(But:** ***sadly*****);** ***red - redder*** **(But:** ***redness*****);** ***ship - shipping*** **(But:** ***shipment*****)**

(2) **Polysyllabic words:** The above rule applies to the final syllable in a polysyllabic word if the final syllable is accented.

Examples: ***admit\′- admitting, admitted*** **(accent on the final syllable of admit)**
confer\′- conferring - conference **(note the shift in accent)**
en\′ter - entering - entered **(accent on the first syllable; no doubling necessary)**

NOTE: Students in the primary grades will not need to know this rule. In addition, most new dictionaries are allowing doubling or non-doubling, as in *travel - traveled/travelled.*

c. **Base words ending in *y*:** When a base word ends with *y*, change the *y* to *i* before adding a suffix.

Examples: *carry - carried; tiny - tinier; try - tried*

(1) Unless the *y* is preceded by a vowel

Examples: *play - player; enjoy - enjoyed; journey - journeyed*

(2) Unless the suffix begins with an *i* (e.g., *-ing, -ish, -ist*)

Examples: *fly - flying; baby - babyish; copy - copyist*

Syllable Division

NOTE: V = vowel; C = consonant. Only the most common patterns are given.

a. **VC/CV closed syllable:** Divide between the two consonants. The vowel in the first syllable usually has the short sound (considered a closed syllable) or the schwa sound (unaccented vowel sound), depending on which syllable is accented.

Examples: *rab/bit, ten/nis, sup/pose, com/mute*

NOTE: Consonant digraphs (i.e., two consonants representing one speech sound, such as *sh, ch, th,* and *wh*, are considered as single consonants in syllable division, as in *ath/lete*).

b. **V/CV open syllable:** The consonant usually goes with the second syllable. The vowel in the first syllable has the long sound or the schwa sound, depending on which syllable is accented.

Examples: *pi/lot, mu/sic, ba/con, he/ro, si/phon* (long vowel)

di/vide, pa/rade, po/lite (schwa sound)

c. **VC/V closed syllable:** Less frequently, the consonant goes with the first syllable and the vowel sound is short.

Examples: *cab/in, lev/el, meth/od*

d. **VC/CCV or VCC/CV:** The syllable division occurs between the consonant and the blend, keeping the blend together.

Examples: *mon/ster, pil/grim pump/kin, port/hole*

Plurals

a. Most nouns are changed to the plural form by adding *s*.

Examples: ***bats, pigs, girls, radios***

b. Nouns ending in *s*, *x*, *z*, *ch*, and *sh* add *es* for the plural. The student will be able to hear the additional syllable formed by the ending.

Examples: ***dresses, foxes, churches, wishes***

c. Nouns ending in *y* form the plural according to the regular suffix addition rule. That is, change the final *y* to *i* and add *es*. If the letter *y* follows a vowel, then keep the *y* and add *s*.

Examples: ***fly - flies; cherry - cherries; toy - toys; chimney - chimneys***

d. Exceptions exist for some nouns ending in *f* or *fe* when they change to *ves*

Examples: ***shelf - shelves; leaf - leaves; wife - wives***

or when they end in *o* and sometimes add *es* (check the dictionary to confirm).

Examples: ***veto - vetoes; tomato - tomatoes; mango - mangoes***

e. Some plurals are completely irregular. Most of them can be spelled correctly by using their sound sequences for clues.

Examples: ***foot - feet; mouse - mice; man - men***

Resources

Historical Perspectives of Written English

American Heritage Dictionary (4th ed.). (2000). Boston: Houghton Mifflin.

Balmuth, M. (2009). *The roots of phonics* (Rev. ed.). Baltimore: Brookes.

Barnett, L. (1965). *The treasure of our tongue.* New York: Knopf.

Claiborne, R. (1983). *Our marvelous native tongue: The life and times of the English language.* New York: Times Books.

Nist, J. (1966). *A structural history of English.* New York: St. Martin's Press.

Historical Perspectives of Written English for Children

Brook, D., & Zallinger, J. D. (Illus.). (1998). *The journey of English.* New York: Clarion Books.

Klausner, J. C. (1990). *Talk about English: How words travel and change.* New York: Crowell.

Krensky, S. (1996). *Breaking into print: Before and after the invention of the printing press.* Toronto: Little, Brown.

Samoyault, T. (1996). *Alphabetical order: How the alphabet began.* New York: Penguin.

Supplementary Materials for Teachers

Bowen, C. (1972). *Angling for words.* Novato, CA: Academic Therapy Publications.

Ehrlich, I. (1988). *Instant vocabulary* (Reissue ed.) New York: Pocket Books. (Excellent for Latin and Greek word roots and affixes.)

Fry, E. B., Polk, J. D., & Fountoukidis, D. L. (1996). *The new reading teacher's book of lists* (3rd ed.). Upper Saddle River, NJ: Prentice Hall.

Henry, M. K., & Redding, N. C. (2004). *Patterns for success in reading and spelling.* Austin, TX: PRO-ED.

Steere, A., Peck, C. Z., & Kahn, L. (1971). *Solving language difficulties.* Cambridge, MA: Educators Publishing Service.

Web Sites of Interest for Words and Language

www.Dictionary-Thesaurus.com

www.oed.com

www.realspelling.com

www.vocabulary.com

www.wordsmith.org/awad/index.html

www.wordworkskingston.com

www.worldwidewords.org

References

Berninger, V. W., & Wolf, B. (2009). *Teaching students with dyslexia and dysgraphia: Lessons for teaching and science.* Baltimore: Brookes.

Calfee, R. C., & Associates. (1981). *The book: Components of reading instruction.* Unpublished manuscript, Stanford University, California.

Calfee, R. C., & Henry, M. K. (1986). Project READ: An inservice model for training classroom teachers in effective reading instruction. In J. V. Hoffman (Ed.), *The effective teaching of reading: Research into practice* (pp.199–229). Newark, DE: International Reading Association.

Ehri, L. (2004). Teaching phonemic awareness and phonics: An explanation of the National Reading Panel meta-analyses. In P. McCardle & V. Chhabra (Eds.), *The voice of evidence in reading research* (pp. 153–186). Baltimore: Brookes.

Gillingham, A., & Stillman, B. (1956). *Remedial training for children with specific disability in reading, spelling and penmanship* (5th ed.). Cambridge, MA: Educators Publishing Service.

Henry, M. K. (1988). Understanding English orthography: Assessment and instruction for decoding and spelling (Doctoral dissertation, Stanford University, 1987). *Dissertation Abstracts International, 48*(11).

Henry, M. K. (2003). *Unlocking literacy: Effective decoding and spelling instruction.* Baltimore: Brookes.

Mathes, P. G., Denton, C. A., Fletcher, J. M., Anthony, J. L., Francis, D. J., & Schatschneider, C. (2005). The effects of theoretically different instruction and student characteristics on the skills of struggling readers. *Reading Research Quarterly, 40*(2), 148–183.

McCardle, P., & Chhabra, V. (2004). *The voice of evidence in reading research.* Baltimore: Brookes.

National Reading Panel. (2000). *Teaching children to read: An evidence-based assessment of the scientific research literature on reading and its implications for reading instruction* (NIH Publication No. 00-4754). Washington, DC: U.S. Government Printing Office.

Shaywitz, S. (2003). *Overcoming dyslexia.* New York: Knopf.

Silliman, E. R., Bahr, R. H., & Peters, M. L. (2006). Spelling patterns in preadolescents with atypical language skills: Phonological, morphological, and orthographic factors. *Developmental Neuropsychology, 20,* 93–123.

Torgesen, J. K. (2004). Lessons learned from research on interventions for students who have difficulty learning to read. In P. McCardle & V. Chhabra (Eds.), *The voice of evidence in reading research* (pp. 355–382). Baltimore: Brookes.

Vaughn, S., & Linan-Thompson, S. (2003). Group size and time allotted to intervention: Effects for students with learning difficulties. In B. Foorman (Ed.), *Preventing and remediating reading difficulties: Bringing science to scale* (pp. 299–324). Baltimore: York Press.